Straight A's

COLLEGE

COOKBOOK

QUICK COOKING *for* 1 *or* 2

Dedication

For my sister, Lauren Applebaum,
and my son, Thor Sigurdson,
my most enthusiastic supporters.

Karen Wokes

Pictured on cover
Chicken and Beef Fajitas, page 105

Straight A's College Cookbook
by
Karen Wokes

First Printing – February 2004

Canadian Cataloguing in Publication Data

Wokes, Karen

Straight A's college cookbook : quick cooking for 1 or 2 /
Karen Wokes ; Patricia Holdsworth, photographer.

Includes index.
ISBN 1-894022-94-7

1. Quick and easy cookery.   2. Cookery for one.   3. Cookery for two.   I. Title.

TX833.5.W64 2004   641.5'55   C2004-900581-2

Photography by: Patricia Holdsworth
    Patricia Holdsworth Photography, Regina, Saskatchewan

Cover and Page Design by: Brian Danchuk
    Brian Danchuk Design, Regina, Saskatchewan

Dishes and Accessories courtesy of:
    Sandstone Gift Essentials
    Gimli, Manitoba R0C 1B0
    (204) 642-9020   FAX (204) 642-9030

Page Formatting and Index by Iona Glabus

Designed, Printed and Produced in Canada by:
Centax Books, a Division of PrintWest Communications Ltd.
Publishing Director, Photo Designer and Food Stylist: Margo Embury
1150 Eighth Avenue, Regina, Saskatchewan, Canada S4R 1C9
(306) 525-2304   FAX (306) 757-2439
E-mail: centax@printwest.com   www.centaxbooks.com

TABLE OF CONTENTS

Recipes have been tested in U.S. Standard measurements. Common metric measurements are given as a convenience for those who are more familiar with metric. Recipes have not been tested in metric.

Straight A's

FOR PLANNING – SHOPPING – COOKING AND CREATIVITY PLUS BONUS MARKS FOR EFFORT (YOURS!)

Most of us are cooking for 1, 2 and sometimes 3. It is a challenge to prepare meals when most recipes are designed for 4 or 6, and most food is packaged for 4 or 6.

The recipes in this cookbook are for busy students, singles, couples, roommates, empty nesters, seniors, and single parents with one child or maybe two. These recipes are healthy, economical, quick to cook, use minimum equipment, for easy cleanup, and include readily available ingredients.

As I promoted my first cookbook, *Quick Cooking for Busy People*, in cities from Calgary and Edmonton to Toronto and Ottawa, people told me over and over that they wanted a cookbook for 1 or 2. They did not want to divide or to be constantly changing recipes. This cookbook is for the people I spoke to and for people who like to plan and cook one meal at a time. It is also for people who prefer to cook with a second meal in mind . . . cook once and eat twice.

Most chapters in this book also include a Very Veggie note – **this chapter is loaded with vegetarian choices**. There is also a vegetarian listing in the index. Many of us are vegetarian or partial vegetarian, and all of us have family and friends who are vegetarian. **The index is your guide to fast and fabulous Very Veggie choices**.

The Student-Survival or Big-Batch Cooking chapter is for instant meals at the end of a long day, and also to satisfy those of us who have economy-minded plan-ahead natures . . . cook and enjoy; divide and freeze. Look in this chapter, also, for easy-to-make, company-class combinations for entertaining.

I included a chapter on entertaining because food and friends mean fun. **Sharing a meal with a friend or two is one of life's greatest pleasures**. Sometimes, in our busy lives, we think we don't have time to entertain. We do.

I also hear the lament, "I don't have time to cook." We do have time to cook. It can take less time to make an omelet or a pot of clam chowder than to order the same dish in a restaurant and wait to be served. **As with *Quick Cooking for Busy People*, most of the recipes in *Straight A's* can be prepared in less time than it takes to have a pizza delivered**.

The key is planning. I have included ideas and planning and shopping strategies to make sure that you always have good food on hand for breakfasts, lunches and SUPER-QUICK MEALS. Planning and shopping are good investments in time, money and healthy eating.

Straight A's is designed for your everyday use, with an emphasis on good food, ingenious short cuts, healthy eating hints and nutrition notes. For new cooks, young and old, the added bonus of kitchen equipment and pantry essentials lists, food storage and food safety tips – all the basics – make *Straight A's* a must-have cookbook.

EAT BETTER & SAVE

Cooking for yourself means that **you save money**, lots of it. **You also eat healthier.**

When you are cooking for yourself you are at an advantage, you can eat what you like and when you like. You do yourself an enormous flavor by eating well. Living alone and eating alone we tend to forget how easy it is to prepare a good meal. Besides providing good nutrition, **cooking for one can be satisfying and creative.**

Most of the recipes in this book are for single servings, ideal for when you are cooking for yourself, when cooking suits your busy come-and-go lifestyle. **Most recipes are also super-quick**, almost-instant. Some dishes are full meals and others invite the addition of a salad or a vegetable. The balance of the recipes are for two or more servings. One to eat, one to share or keep for a second meal. **A meal stored is an investment.**

Good meals don't just happen. They take a little preparation and time. **Plan a little** – spend an hour a week shopping and 20 to 30 minutes a day preparing a meal. Three meals and snacks, 365 days of the year, is a big responsibility. Take it seriously – you'll also have fun and feel a great sense of accomplishment.

If you think you can't or don't like to cook, learn. You will eat better, cheaper and healthier. **Hamburgers and chicken can be prepared at home for about a quarter of what you pay at a fast-food outlet – less fat and NO TAXES.**

Buy a minimum of processed and packaged food. Grate your own cheese, wash your own lettuce and season your food yourself. Fancy foil packages of fajita seasonings or pasta sauce flavorings are basically salt, cornstarch or flour as thickeners, spices and herbs. Maybe 20 cents worth for $1.00-$2.00 – make your own.

Eat less meat, which is expensive; eat more beans and grains, which are nutritious and cheap. Eat at least one meatless meal a week.

Know the value of foods that you like and buy them when they are on sale. Make them part of your weekly meal plan. Buy basics like potatoes, onions and carrots in larger quantities. They store and keep well in the fridge.

Occasionally, cook in large batches. A slow cooker can be your best friend, or at least cook your best meals. Soups, stews and chilies loaded with vegetables, beans and broth (meat too) are full of good nutrition. Divided, packaged and frozen they promise easy access to meals for the days ahead. Freezer-quality resealable bags are excellent for storage. They are reasonably priced, convenient, easily labeled and stored. The contents can be partially thawed in the microwave or warm water, ready to heat and eat or combine with other ingredients.

GOOD EATING

- **Eat what you enjoy most.** Be sure to include seasonal favorites like spring asparagus, summer peas and new potatoes, autumn tomatoes, winter squash and root vegetables.

- **Invite a friend to share a meal.** You will eat better and it adds incentive to meal preparation. Besides, then you'll also get invited out for a meal.

- **Plan a potluck** with a group of friends, spend the evening together and enjoy the good conversation and good food. Have half the group bring a main course or salad and the others appetizers, beverage and dessert.

- **Identify "instant" meals in your cookbooks**; mark them with tabs. This becomes a quick reference when you don't know what to prepare. Better yet, choose a meal idea from this book – **most of the recipes are super-quick, 20-30 minutes or less**.

- Make time to **try new recipes** or try to make a restaurant favorite at home.

- For good eating and convenience, **make enough salad for 2 servings**, Make it directly into 2 bowls, one for NOW and one for tomorrow's lunch or supper. Cover the second salad and add the dressing when you eat it.

- **Always cook extra rice**, ground meat, chili, soup and stew; divide into serving sizes and store.

- **Fruits and vegetables**, and more fruits and vegetables, are easy, nutritious additions to all your meals.

- When you **shop the bulk food bins** in the supermarket or health food store you can choose the exact amount of what you want in grains, rice, legumes, flours, cereals, pastas, dried fruits and nuts, baking ingredients, herbs and spices. They are usually less expensive and also fresher. Candies and snacks can be bought this way too.

- **Choose smaller packages** of pre-packaged vegetables at the supermarket or ask the clerk to rebundle. Some stores have a salad-bar-like presentation of vegetables and fruits. Fruits and vegetables are easy nutritious additions to all your meals.

- **Rely on some basic convenience foods** such as washed-and-ready-to-eat salads, prepared meats and vegetables, canned beans, tomatoes, tuna and salmon.

- **Choose individual portions** of puddings, canned fruits, cheese and yogurts, single-serving soups and small cans of vegetables, baked beans, chili and fish.

- **Small bags** of frozen vegetables and fruits are especially convenient. Make baby green peas, kernel corn, blueberries, loose frozen raspberries and sliced peaches essentials on your shopping list.

- **The freezer section** has lots of wonderfully convenient foods all individually frozen. Look for shrimp, chicken, fish fillets, vegetable pasta mixes and Tex Mex favorites like burritos.

- **Check out the deli counter** for ready-cooked meals or for an "add to" for on-hand ingredients.

HEALTHY EATING

For better health, do not skip meals. Research shows that several small meals a day help the body and brain work more efficiently than having 1 or 2 big meals a day.

- **Eat more grains** – use combinations of grains and vegetables instead of meat as a main dish.
- When cooking pork and beef, **choose lean cuts and eat smaller amounts**. Remove skin from chicken breasts, legs and thighs.
- **Choose low-fat** or no-fat dairy products.
- **Cut down on** the amount of **salt and** refined (white) **sugar** in your diet, and limit your consumption of products containing them.
- **Drink 6 to 8 glasses of water a day.** Coffee, tea and soft drinks don't count. Limit their consumption.
- **Eat more fiber!** High-fiber foods help to give you that satisfied feeling. They play an important role in the prevention of cancer and heart disease. Fruits, vegetables, beans, lentils, whole-wheat products, grains and brown rice are good sources of fiber.
- Use non-stick cooking pans and **reduce the amount of oil or fat you use for cooking**. Try spraying the pan with oil rather than using the amount specified in a recipe.

PLANNING & SHOPPING

Do it your way but do it! **Good shopping is the key to good eating.** Meal planning with every detail and every ingredient listed on paper is not my style. Making lists is. I keep basics like pastas, grains, canned fish, tomatoes and sauces, herbs and spices on hand, and shop weekly for meat, fish and fresh produce. I make my list from the weekly specials in store flyers or as displayed in the store. I include seasonal specials and my particular favorites, such as salmon or asparagus. **Eating well is a big responsibility and very much worth a little time and energy.**

- To avoid frustration when shopping in the MEGA supermarkets, **group your food needs and organize your list into store sections**. Fresh meats and produce are on the outside walls, add them to your cart last.

- **Keep a well-stocked pantry of basics** and a shopping list handy (in the same place all the time) so you can add items as needed.

- **Shop regularly**, once a week or every 3 to 4 days. Try to shop at non-peak times, early morning or late evening. Shop for healthy meals and snacks. Learn to read the nutrition and ingredient labels on packaged foods.

- **Look for new ideas and products.** Many neighborhoods have wonderful markets with single-serving prepared foods to go. Try an Italian, Greek, Mediterranean, Indian, Thai or Chinese take-home.

- Planning helps and makes life easier, but plans change. **There is always room for spontaneity**, a meal out or the inclusion of an impromptu picnic or treat.

FOOD GUIDE TO HEALTHY EATING

(For People Age 4 and Over) Different People Need Different Amounts of Food:

The amount of food you need every day from the 4 food groups and other foods depends on your age, body size, activity level, whether you are male or female and if you are pregnant or breast-feeding. That's why the Food Guide gives a lower and higher number of servings for each food group, e.g., young children can choose the lower number of servings, while male teenagers can go to the higher number. Most other people can choose servings somewhere in between.

GRAIN PRODUCTS
5 to 12 Servings per day

1 Serving: 1 slice of toast; 1 oz. (30 g) cold cereal;
$^3/_4$ cup (175 mL) hot cereal
2 Servings: 1 bagel, pita or bun; 1 cup (250 mL) pasta or rice

VEGETABLES & FRUIT
5 to 10 Servings per day

1 Serving: 1 medium-size vegetable or fruit; $^1/_2$ cup (125 mL) fresh, frozen or canned vegetables or fruit; 1 cup (250 mL) salad; $^1/_2$ cup (125 mL) juice

MILK PRODUCTS
5 to 10 Servings per day

1 Serving: 1 cup (250 mL) milk; 1 x 1 x 3" (50 g) cheese; 2 (50 g) cheese slices; $^3/_4$ cup (175 mL) yogurt

MEAT/ALTERNATIVES
2 to 3 Servings per day

1 Serving 50-100 g meat. poultry or fish; 1 to 2 eggs; $^1/_3$-$^2/_3$ can (50-100 g) canned fish; $^1/_3$ cup (100 g) cheese $^1/_2$-1 cup (125-250 mL) beans; 2 tbsp. (30 mL) peanut butter;

OTHER FOODS: Taste and enjoyment can also come from foods and beverages not part of the 4 food groups, e.g., snack foods. Some are higher in fat or calories, so use these foods in moderation.

Enjoy a variety of foods from each group every day. Choose lower-fat foods more often.

GRAINS: Choose whole-grain and enriched products..

VEGETABLES & FRUIT: Choose dark green and orange vegetables and orange fruit more often.

MILK PRODUCTS: Choose lower-fat milk products.

MEAT/ALTERNATIVES: Eat less meat. Choose leaner meats, poultry and fish, as well as dried peas, beans and lentils more often.

The Best Diet

- **Eat Well – Eat Less – Move More**

- **Live a balanced life – Eat a balanced diet**

PANTRY ESSENTIALS

The recipes in this book are created to include a minimum of ingredients and take a minimum amount of time to prepare. I have included almost no commercial sauces, expensive flavoring or condiment packets. Most of those products, which are placed to catch your eye in the supermarket, contain fillers such as cornstarch, preservatives, loads of salt and a few herbs and spices. They have little or no food value, clutter the fridge and cupboard and produce pangs of guilt when not used. **Good things to keep on hand, to add flavor and variety to your meals are herbs, spices, vinegars, flavored oils and fresh vegetables and fruits, especially lemons and limes.**

Here is a list of essentials and good things to eat that will help you cook your recipe choices quickly and inexpensively.

ON HAND

Baking powder
Baking soda
Cereals – dried, ready-to-eat and quick-cooking oatmeal
Cocoa powder
Coffee and tea
Cornstarch
Couscous
Dried fruits and nuts – apricots, dates, raisins, cranberries, peanuts, pecans, almonds and pine nuts
Evaporated milk
Flour – white, unbleached all-purpose and whole-wheat
Grains, beans and lentils
Pasta – 2 or 3 of your favorite kinds
Peanut butter, honey, jams and jellies (all-fruit varieties have less sugar)
Rice – regular long-grain white, quick-cooking white and brown
Soy sauce – reduced sodium
Sugar – brown, white
Vegetable oil – olive oil, canola
Vegetables and fruits – potatoes, onions, carrots, garlic, celery, tomatoes, grapefruit, oranges, apples, bananas, pears
Vinegars – white, cider, red wine, balsamic

CONDIMENTS & SEASONINGS

Dried herbs and spices – salt, pepper, cinnamon, nutmeg, oregano, Italian mixed herbs, garlic powder, red pepper flakes, chili powder, curry powder or paste, cumin, dillweed, thyme, rosemary
Hot pepper sauce, Worcestershire sauce, squeeze-bottle pizza sauce
Mayonnaise – low-fat
Mustards – Dijon-style, American
Salad dressings – low-fat
Salsa and ketchup
Teriyaki sauce (reduced sodium) or Sweet and Sour Sauce

CANNED GOODS

Beans, lentils, chickpeas
Broths – chicken, beef, vegetable
Fruits
Juices
Meat and fish – chicken, ham, tuna, salmon, clams
Pasta, pizza sauces
Tomatoes, tomato paste, sauce
Soups, chili

IN THE FREEZER

California vegetables
Pasta veggie mixes
Peas, corn, green beans
Fruit – blueberries, strawberries, raspberries, peaches

SHOPPING FOR CONVENIENCE & GOOD NUTRITION

To save cooking and shopping time, and to eat well, know what your supermarket has to offer.

Search for appealing foods that are packaged in 1 or 2 servings. For best nutrition and value, **look for what I call "real food"**, products that have a minimum of salt, additives, processing and expensive packaging.

DELICATESSENS

- 3-bean salad, pasta and rice salads, potato salad, coleslaws, Greek salad, antipastos, and Thai or Chinese noodles
- A wide choice of cooked meat and poultry
- Processed meats, ham, turkey, salami
- Roasted chicken – whole, halves or quarters

In the supermarkets, delicatessens and specialty stores and restaurants you will find an amazing variety of prepared take-home meals. they are a good choice for once in a while but too expensive and not the best nutrition choice for every day.

FROZEN FOODS

- Small bags of fruits and veggies – shake out what you need and store the remainder.
- Try carrots, corn, Brussels sprouts, peas, broccoli and veggie combos.
- Look for strawberries, raspberries, blueberries, peaches and fruit combos.
- Veggie and pasta combinations are flavorful, quick to cook and an almost-instant accompaniment to chicken, meat or a salad.
- Perogies, pre-shaped buns, pizza bases
- Ready-to-bake pizzas, cooked chicken and ribs, chicken or beef pot pies, shepherd's pie, quiche, lasagne, even tourtière
- Tart and pie crusts

PRODUCE

- Precut salad bar veggies and vegetables displayed individually – celery stalks, cauliflower and broccoli florets
- Shredded cabbage and broccoli florets in bags
- Prewashed salad mixtures and spinach in bags

DAIRY CASE AND REFRIGERATED YOU-BAKE ITEMS

- Yogurt and yogurt-fruit combinations
- Refrigerated puddings
- Shredded and sliced cheese, reduced-fat cheeses
- Bake-at-home cookies, biscuits, cinnamon rolls, pizza bases, bread sticks and apple or blueberry turnovers

SINGLE-SERVING CANNED FOOD

- Deep-brown beans, chili and pasta
- Puddings and fruit
- Tuna, salmon, chicken and ham
- Chunky soups
- Vegetable, tomato and fruit juices
- Small cans of pasta and pizza sauce
- Sandwich Mate singles 2¹/₂ oz. (65 g) size, complete with mayo and seasoning
- Tuna salad, complete with crackers and a spreader. There are several types.
- Salmon and tuna antipasto snacks

Cook's Tip

Limit the number of extras that you buy, things like prepackaged seasonings, mixes and bottles of sauces. They have little food value and usually contain many additives. It is surprising how much those "little extras" cost and how much they can inflate the total on the checkout tape.

EQUIPMENT & TOOLS

A single cook's needs are a little different from a family cook's. Sometimes, the single cook is faced with the minimum in a small apartment, including an old fridge, no oven or an inaccurate one. In that case, a low-cost toaster oven will toast, roast, bake and broil, and generally fill the need for an oven. A poor fridge will mean careful shopping and keeping a minimum amount of food on hand at one time. A microwave is almost a necessity for quick meal preparation and easy reheats. Buy one with at least 1,000 watts power and medium-to-large capacity (1.3 cubic feet).

EQUIPMENT AND TOOLS

- 3 bowls, small, medium and large – choose a nesting set of glass ovenproof bowls
- 2 glass casseroles with flat lids, 2-cup (500 mL) and 1½-quart (1.5 L) sizes, the flat lids can double as oven, microwave and serving dishes
- **Buy good-quality, medium-priced cookware.** They last longer and work better. Choose a 1½-quart (1.5 liter) saucepan with a lid and a 5-6-quart (5-6 L) saucepan with lid, non-stick if you like.
- Colander for draining pasta
- Small non-stick frying pan/skillet
- Medium non-stick frying pan/skillet, lids for these 2 pans are useful, usually your pot lids can do double duty – they don't have to fit exactly
- A medium-sized metal strainer – doubles as a flour sifter
- 2-cup (500 mL) shallow ovenproof casserole or gratin dishes for oven-to-table meals and for serving dishes (Check your dishes, they will say if they are ovenproof and microwaveable. It is a real bonus when they are.)

Cook's Tips

Use elastic bands or metal clips to keep your cookbooks open when in use.

Keep your knives sharp – they will be easier to use and safer, too.

Don't put your non-stick pans in the dishwasher. The chemicals and abrasives in dish detergents are very hard on the non-stick finish.

BAKING & GENERAL KITCHEN USE

- When buying baking pans, cookie sheets and muffin pans **choose good-quality mid-priced pieces**. The inexpensive pans do not bake as well and they rust.

- 1 baking pan 8" (20 cm) square – can double as a pan for meat and chicken dishes

- 1 cookie pan/sheet 12 x 18" (30 x 45 cm) or 11 x 15" (28 x 38 cm) – 2 if you are into serious cookie making

- 1 round layer cake pan 9" (23 cm)

- 1, $4^1/_2$ x 9" (11 x 23 cm)" loaf pan or $3^1/_2$ x $7^1/_2$" (9 x 19 cm)

- 1 small pie pan 7" (18 cm) or 8" (20 cm)

- 1 standard 6-cup muffin pan

- 2" (5 cm) or 3" (8 cm) cookie/biscuit cutter

- Set of measuring cups and measuring spoons

- Cutting boards – 2 or 3, different sizes

- 2-cup (500 mL) glass measuring cup – for measuring and for microwave use

- Rolling pin (a cylinder-type wine bottle will do in a pinch)

- Pot holders, tea towels, 1 or 2 small hand towels and dish cloths

- Trivets for hot pots and casseroles, suitable for the table and the counter top

- Pot cleaner/scraper

NICE TO HAVE:

- Cooling racks for cookies and cakes

- Electric hand mixer

- Kitchen scale, a small inexpensive diet scale is fine

- 2-3-quart (2-3 L) enameled cast-iron casserole with lid, for roasts, stews, chilies – it goes from stove-top or oven to table

- Instant-read thermometer

UTENSILS

- Spoons, salad servers, spatulas, a ladle and tongs – wooden spatulas and stirrers are nice to work with and good for your non-stick pans

- Heatproof vinyl spatulas do double duty as stirrers and scrapers

- Kitchen scissors, a good-quality can opener and a vegetable peeler that works

- Good knives are essential and make food preparation and cooking much easier. You will need a knife sharpener as well. Choose 3 knives – a medium-sized French or all-purpose knife, a paring knife and a serrated bread knife. I also like a medium-sized all-purpose knife for slicing meats and for general use.

- Small and medium-sized wire whisks – No whisk? Use a fork!

- Good-quality 4-sided grater for shredding vegetables and cheese

- Cork screw

- Garlic press

- Pump-style oil spray – this is an essential. Half fill the pump with your favorite oil and use when cooking with non-stick pans or for coating bakeware and casseroles.

NICE TO HAVE

- Pastry blender – so handy when making biscuits

- Blender

- Slow cooker

- Food processor

SUPPLIES

- Waxed paper

- Aluminum foil

- Paper towels

- Plastic wrap

- Plastic food-storage bags and lunch bags

- Parchment paper – use to cover pan when making cookies or baking chicken fingers for no-mess clean up.

Cook's Tip

Kitchen scissors cut almost everything – small amounts of salad greens and herbs, stems off spinach and the spinach leaves. Use them to open pitas and to cut tortillas and pitas in halves and quarters. Be sure to wash the scissors before you use them.

FOOD SAFETY

Keeping food safe to eat is part of the good cook's role. There are just four rules: keep it clean, keep hot foods hot, cold foods cold, and store food appropriately.

KEEP IT CLEAN

- Keep the kitchen clean with hot soapy water, including counter tops, appliances, cupboard shelves, fridge interior and door-handle and storage containers.

- **Wash your hands often** and make sure others working with food also wash theirs. Cover any cuts or infections with a bandage or rubber gloves.

- When you are working quickly and preparing a multi-step meal, keep a bowl of warm soapy water close by for quick hand rinsing.

- **Wash cutting boards and knives frequently** with soap and hot water. Rinse well. Store the boards upright on the counter to dry.

- Change kitchen cloths and sponges daily. Wash kitchen towels often.

- Wash, rinse and dry all produce, even "prewashed".

- Never eat raw chicken, meat or fish.

- After using a plate for raw meat, poultry or fish, wash the plate with hot soapy water before reusing or use a clean plate to serve the meat.

KEEP HOT FOODS HOT

- Once food has been cooked, serve it hot or cool slightly and refrigerate.

- **The maximum time for keeping food at room temperature, e.g., buffets or potlucks, is 2 hours. After that discard the food. Do not keep it.**

- Foods standing for more than 1-2 hours should be kept hot in an electric skillet, a chafing dish or on a hot tray.

TAKE-AWAY OR DELI FOODS

Most take-away and deli foods, such as sauced meat and poultry dishes and pasta salads, should be eaten as soon as possible. It is not wise to keep and store the leftovers. Some meals from the deli counter can be served and the remainder stored, for example, vinegar-based coleslaws and marinated salads can be stored in the fridge. If you are not sure, ask the store employee.

Creamy salads and most cooked entrées should not be left at room temperature and then refrigerated. They must be discarded.

Refrigerated leftovers not used within 2 days should be discarded.

When in doubt, throw it out!

KEEP COLD FOODS COLD

- **Foods intended to be cold can be kept at room temperature for only 2 hours, or less, before they become unsafe to eat.** Wrap and refrigerate leftovers immediately after a meal. Refrigerator temperature should be 34 to 40°F (1 to 4°C). Refrigeration retards bacteria growth – it does not stop it. Remember the 2-day rule: small amounts of food not used within 2 days are discarded.

- When shopping, **purchase meats and dairy foods last** and package them together in the same grocery bags. Refrigerate as soon as possible, particularly in the summer. Cars are hot.

- **Frozen foods are best thawed in the refrigerator or the microwave.** For fridge thawing, place the frozen package in the fridge the night before or in the morning. If the package is not completely thawed you may begin cooking. Meats thawed in a microwave should be cooked immediately as parts of the meat have usually begun to cook.

FOOD STORAGE AND HANDLING

- **Cover and refrigerate leftovers immediately after each meal.** Food cools more quickly on the open wire shelves of the refrigerator than on the solid bottom shelf.

- For safe chicken, meat and fish handling, refrigerate as soon as possible after purchase. **When ready to use, open the packages over the sink.** Dispose of the wrappings in the garbage immediately, and place the meat, chicken or fish on a clean plate, or process or cook immediately. If the meat, etc., or wrappings come in contact with the sink, wash the sink and rinse it immediately.

- **When using leftovers, reheat until very hot.**

FOOD SAFETY OUTDOORS

When serving food at a picnic, or at a rest stop on a long car trip, be food wise and ready for quick cleanups.

- **Wash your hands often.** For picnics and similar excursions, pack a bag with hand-washing and tidy-up needs. Include some or all of these: pre-moistened towelettes, such as baby wipes; pre-moistened or soaped face cloths in a plastic bag; a small towel or paper towels; a bottle of water; waterless hand-sanitizing lotion.

- **Use your coolers to the maximum.** Freeze or chill food thoroughly before placing in the cooler. Use ice packs or frozen juice boxes to pack around the food. No ice packs? Fill empty milk cartons with water, freeze overnight and use as ice packs. Fill cooler to the top – cold things keep cold things cold. If the cooler is not quite full, cover the food with several layers of newspaper for insulation.

- If you have two coolers, use one for items like meats and pasta or potato salads; use the other for items often accessed, like fruit, vegetables and drinks. Find a shady spot to store the coolers.

- **Keep raw meats and ready-to-eat foods separate**. Use separate plates for raw and cooked meats. Take extra plastic grocery bags to transport used plates and utensils. Be sure to have separate cutting boards and areas for meat products and breads and vegetables.

- **Cook foods to proper/safe temperatures**. Harmful bacteria are destroyed when meats are cooked to safe temperatures. Learn how to determine if food is cooked adequately and/or use an instant-read thermometer (see page 109).

- **Store leftovers properly**. In hot weather, more than 80°F (27°C), any perishable food that has been out of the cooler for an hour or more should be discarded. Perishable foods that you wish to keep for another serving should be refrigerated or chilled as soon as possible. Keep and refrigerate only the foods that were not sitting outside the cooler. Refrigeration slows the growth of bacteria, it does not stop it. What you don't use the next day should be discarded.

POULTRY

Remember to **use warm soapy water to immediately wash all surfaces that come into contact with raw poultry**. Knives, utensils and hands too! When the cleanup is complete, rinse the cloth out and put it into the laundry. Hang it over the edge of the basket to dry, otherwise it will stay moist and provide a home for bacteria growth.

FOR FREEZING

When meat is purchased to be stored and frozen, use these guidelines to maintain quality.

- Meat purchased in heat-sealed transparent film can be frozen as is for up to 2 weeks, provided the wrapping is not pierced.

- For longer storage, and if the seal is pierced, place the packages in freezer bags, remove as much air as possible and seal.

- For larger quantities – divide amount into number of servings desired, bag, label and date. When including 2 or more pieces per bag, place waxed paper or plastic film between pieces for easier separation when frozen.

- Well-wrapped meat can be stored in a fridge freezer for a couple of months – longer in a chest freezer. **But – don't store it, use it.**

KITCHEN FIRES

PREVENTION

- Never leave papers, tea towels or cloths on or near the stove.
- Use potholders or oven mitts, not kitchen towels, when handling hot pots and pans. If towels are damp the steam can burn you, and the edges are always at risk of catching fire.
- Never leave a pot on the stove unattended (except for simmering stews).
- Always turn pot and pan handles in, so that they cannot be knocked over or caught on clothing.

TO EXTINGUISH

- If the oil in a skillet ignites, cover it with a pot lid.
- Small flames in an oven or toaster oven or on a stove top can be extinguished with baking soda.
- **Do not try to extinguish larger fires.** Leave the area, apartment or house and call 911.

GENERAL KITCHEN TIPS

- Soak pans with burned-on food in baking soda and water; simmer for 10 minutes before washing.
- To clean out coffee- or tea-stained pots or mugs, scrub them with a paste of baking soda and water.
- For a fresher-smelling fridge or freezer, place an open box of baking soda inside. Replace the soda after 3 months. The used soda can be utilized as a drain cleaner – pour 1/2 cup (125 mL) of baking soda down a slow drain; after a few minutes, flush drain with 2 quarts (2 L) very hot water.
- Baking soda on a damp cloth can be used to wash stained countertops.
- For easy cleaning of your microwave, place a small bowl of water, with a generous squirt of lemon juice, in the microwave. Heat on HIGH for 5-10 minutes. Dried-on food will wipe off with a damp cloth.
- Lemon juice, or the pulpy half of a squeezed lemon, is excellent for cleaning/bleaching stained fingernails and cuticles.

B R E A D S,
B I S C U I T S   &
M U F F I N S

Bonus Biscuits

Biscuits are one of my comfort foods, whether served with homemade soup and cheese or with strawberry jam and a cup of tea. Easy and quick to make, this dough can be adapted to make Cinnamon Rolls, savory biscuits, even a pizza base. Creative comfort food – what could be better?

1 cup	unbleached all-purpose flour	250 mL
2 tsp.	baking powder	10 mL
pinch	salt	pinch
2 tbsp.	cold butter OR shortening	30 mL
1/3-1/2 cup	milk	75-125 mL

- Preheat oven to 425°F (220°C).

- Mix together flour, baking powder and salt. Cut butter into small pieces, and add to flour mixture. Blend with a knife or fingers until pieces are the size of small peas.

- Pour almost all the milk over flour mixture. Stir and mix with a fork. Add a little more milk if necessary.

- Dump flour mixture onto a lightly floured (clean) countertop , knead (mix and turn with your hands) 3 or 4 times, until dough can be patted into a circle.

- Cut into biscuits with a floured cookie cutter or a small can with the top and bottom removed. Place biscuits on a pizza pan or small cookie sheet. Bake until lightly browned, about 12 minutes.

Makes 4 or 5 biscuits, double the recipe for 8-10 biscuits

*H*omemade baked goods, biscuits, quick breads and muffins are more flavorful, nutritious and economical than bakery versions.

Homemade means less fat, less sugar, no preservatives. You can also include healthy extras like whole-wheat flour and wheat germ.

These quick recipes are for small amounts, 5 biscuits or 6 muffins. They can be enjoyed and shared or extra servings can be packaged and frozen for good eating at another time.

Included are ideas for savory breads to serve as super-quick snacks or as "go withs" when you have soups and stews.

Very Veggie – this chapter is loaded with vegetarian choices.

See Variations on next page.

Bonus Biscuits *continued*

Variations

CHEDDAR AND GREEN ONION BISCUITS – Add $1/2$ cup (125 mL) grated **old Cheddar cheese** and 2 **green onions**, chopped (using some of the green part), to the flour mixture. Add **milk**, shape and bake as on page 19. For a **GARLIC PUNCH**, brush the tops of the biscuits with a little **olive oil** and **crushed garlic**.

CHEDDAR HERB BISCUITS – Add $1/2$ cup (125 mL) grated old **Cheddar cheese** and $1/2$ tsp. (2 mL) EACH of **oregano**, **basil** and **thyme** OR **rosemary** and **thyme** or **savory**.

Pictured on page 49

HERB BISCUITS – Omit the cheese.

ITALIAN HERB BISCUITS – Add 1 tbsp. (15 mL) **Italian mixed herbs** and $1/3$-$1/2$ cup (75-125 mL) grated **Parmesan cheese** to the flour mixture on page 19. Add **milk**, shape and bake as in the basic recipe.

CINNAMON ROLL BISCUITS – Make the biscuit dough on page 19. Knead lightly on a floured counter top. Press into a rectangle shape about $1/4$" (6 mm) thick. Spread with **butter or margarine**, **brown sugar** and **cinnamon**, lots of cinnamon. Roll up from the long side cut in 1" (2.5 cm) slices and place in well-greased or oiled muffin cups. Bake in preheated oven at 375°F (190°C) until the rolls are light brown in color, about 15 minutes.

CINNAMON PECAN STICKY BISCUITS – Place 2 tsp. (10 mL) **maple syrup or corn syrup** in each well-greased or oiled muffin cup. Sprinkle with **brown sugar** and **chopped pecans** or **raisins**. Place Cinnamon Roll Biscuits in cups and bake as above.

Cook's Tips

For a quicker version and no counter mess, make drop biscuits. Drop large spoonfuls of biscuit dough onto the baking pan, press down a little and bake as above.

Packaged biscuit mix may also be used to make these biscuits. The biscuit mix is a quick choice for pizza bases and pancakes, too.

SUPER-QUICK SAVORY BREADS

Buttered, flavored and baked for a few minutes, these bakery breads become super-quick savory snacks or welcome accents to soups, chilies and stews.

QUICK GARLIC BREADSTICKS – Complete the baking of packaged, prebaked bread sticks as indicated on the package. Spread generously with **butter OR margarine** and sprinkle with **garlic powder** and a sprinkle of **salt**. Serve immediately.

CHEESY BREAD – Cut a **baguette** in half lengthwise. Cover with **cheese** spread and sprinkle with grated **mozzarella**. Bake at 425°F (220°C) until cheese melts and begins to brown, 8-10 minutes. This is a good use of day-old bread.

CHEESY GARLIC BREAD – Prepare as for Cheesy Bread and sprinkle with **garlic powder** before baking.

Pictured on page 137

PESTO CHEESE BREAD – Spread bread with bottled pesto and top with grated pizza cheese (mozzarella). Bake at 425°F (220°C) until cheese is bubbly, about 8-10 minutes.

SAVORY FOCACCIA – Sprinkle 1/2 tsp. (1.3 cm) of **dried Italian herbs** over an 8" (20 cm) focaccia, sprinkle with 1 cup (250 mL) grated **mozzarella cheese**. Bake at 375° (190°C) until heated through and the cheese melts, 12-15 minutes.

Pictured on page 67

CROÛTONS – Cut 2 or 3 slices of **whole-wheat or French bread** into 1/2" (1.3 cm) cubes. Spray with **olive oil** and sprinkle with **dried Italian herbs** and/or **garlic powder**, if you like. Toast in a toaster oven at 300°F (150°C) for about 10 minutes; stir and toast for 10 minutes more.

CROSTINI – Toast thin fresh or leftover **baguette slices** to make wonderful crostini for bruschetta spreads and cheeses. For added flavor, brush slices with **olive oil** before toasting.

Cook's Tips

Use French bread slices, a bun or English muffin halves to make **croûtons**. This is also the best way to use up less than fresh bread. Delicious!

The small, 8" (20 cm) focaccia, flat breads, tortillas and pizza bases all fit in toaster ovens. Use the oven to heat the breads or to make pizzas, melts, quesadillas and toasted sandwiches.

Baguettes are low-fat or no-fat (without the butter) – that's the good news, but they don't keep well. When you have leftovers, cut the loaf in very thin 1/4-1/2" (6 mm-1.3 cm) slices and toast in a 300°F (150°C) oven for 10 minutes to make **crostini**. Cool and store in a plastic bag.

Veggie Rolls

My favorite coffee shop serves a veggie roll. When I am on the road selling books or travelling to visit my grandchildren, it is my choice for a quick lunch. I decided to try making them at home and found that they were easy, quick to make and delicious, too.

Bonus Biscuit Dough, page 19, knead till smooth and pat into a rectangle about 7 x 9" (15 x 23 cm).

Spread with 1 of the following combos:

Filling Options

- **Pasta sauce**, grated **Cheddar cheese**.

- **Cheese spread**, finely chopped, cooked **broccoli or asparagus**, grated medium **Cheddar cheese** . . . 1/2 cup (125 mL) veggies and 1/2 cup (125 mL) cheese is ample.

- **Pesto sauce** and sautéed, finely chopped **mushrooms** and **onions** – add a little **garlic,** too.

- **Italian salad dressing** and finely grated **carrots**.

- Mash the beans in leftover **chili**; spread chili on dough, add grated **Cheddar cheese**.

- **Cheese spread**, thin slices of deli **ham**, grated **Cheddar cheese** and a few **spinach leaves**, if you have them.

- Preheat oven to 400°F (200°C).

- Place dough on a lightly floured counter and spread, gently pushing and smoothing with your fingers, until the dough is about 1/4" (1 mL) thick. The rest is a little like making a pizza. Spread with 1 of the filling options; roll up and cut into 1 1/2" (4 cm) slices. Here, less is better. **Don't overload**. You want the dough tender-crisp, not soaked with juices.

- Oil a medium-sized 6-cup muffin pan and place rolls in the muffin cups, cut side down.

- Bake for 15-20 minutes. Keep watch after about 15 minutes – the cooking time will depend on the size and density of the rolls.

Makes 4-5 rolls

Cook's Tips

Packaged biscuit mix can be used to make the dough. Biscuit mix is a quick choice for pizzas and pancakes, too! Follow the package directions.

When you have an empty muffin cup, pour a bit of water into it to prevent any damage to the pan.

Blueberry Muffins

Low-fat and delicious, this recipe makes 6 muffins.

1 cup	unbleached all-purpose flour	250 mL
2 tsp.	baking powder	10 mL
1/4 tsp.	salt	1 mL
2 tbsp.	sugar	30 mL
1/4 tsp.	nutmeg	1 mL
1	egg	1
1/2 cup	skim milk	125 mL
2 tbsp.	melted butter, margarine OR vegetable oil	30 mL
1/2 cup	fresh or frozen blueberries	125 mL

- Preheat oven to 400°F (200°C)

- Lightly oil a 6-cup muffin pan or line with paper liners, lightly sprayed with oil.

- In a large bowl, combine flour, baking powder, salt, sugar and nutmeg.

- Break the egg into a separate bowl. Add milk and melted butter. Whisk until combined.

- Pour milk mixture into dry mixture. **Stir until just combined**. Add blueberries and stir lightly once or twice. A light touch and a minimum of mixing makes a tender muffin. Spoon batter into muffin pan, filling cups to 2/3 full. Bake 20-25 minutes.

Makes 6 medium muffins. For 12 muffins, double the ingredients.

Variations

WHOLE-WHEAT MUFFINS – Use 1/2 cup (125 mL) unbleached **flour** and 1/2 cup (125 mL) **whole-wheat flour**.

BANANA MUFFINS – Omit blueberries and stir in 1 small **banana** cut into 1/4" (6.3 mm) chunks. Mix a little **cinnamon** and white **sugar** and sprinkle over baked muffins

CHOCOLATE PECAN MUFFINS – Omit nutmeg; add 1/4 tsp. (1 mL) **cinnamon**, 1/3 cup (75 mL) semisweet **chocolate chips** and 1/3 cup (75 mL) coarsely chopped toasted **pecans**.

Nice to add – A little grated **lemon zest,** added to the flour, perks up the flavor of muffins. A mixture of **cinnamon** and **sugar** sprinkled on top of muffins before baking adds flavor and eye appeal.

Nutrition Note

Blueberries have the highest antioxidant activity of any fruits or vegetables. They help prevent urinary tract infections and help reduce eye fatigue. New studies indicate that blueberries are also beneficial in reducing oxidative stress, thereby helping to prevent some cancers, heart disease and Alzheimer's. Start young – eat blueberries!

Pumpkin Raisin Muffins

Low-fat buttermilk and nutritious pumpkin take the place of much of the oil in these moist and spicy muffins. Muffins freeze well and make a great breakfast, snack, or portable lunch, along with some cheese or yogurt and fresh fruit.

1 1/2 cups	unbleached all-purpose flour	375 mL
2 tsp.	baking powder	10 mL
1/2 tsp.	baking soda	2 mL
1 tsp.	cinnamon	5 mL
1/2 tsp.	nutmeg (optional)	2 mL
1/2 tsp.	salt	2 mL
1/2 cup	buttermilk OR sour milk (see note below)	125 mL
1/2 cup	canned pure pumpkin	125 mL
1/4 cup	vegetable oil	60 mL
1/2 cup	brown sugar	125 mL
1	egg	1
1/2 cup	raisins	125 mL

- Preheat oven to 400°F (200°C).

- Grease 12 muffin cups or line with paper liners, lightly sprayed with oil.

- In a large bowl, mix flour, baking powder, baking soda, cinnamon, nutmeg (if using), and salt.

- In a smaller bowl (or 2 cup liquid measure), mix buttermilk, pumpkin, oil, brown sugar, and egg.

- Add liquid ingredients to dry; **stir until just combined**. Stir in raisins.

- Divide batter between 12 muffin cups. Bake 15-18 minutes – a toothpick inserted in the center of a muffin should come out with no batter clinging to it.

- Cool 10 minutes in pan, then remove to rack to cool completely.

Makes 12 muffins

Variation

PUMPKIN ORANGE MUFFINS – Follow the method given above. Substitute 1/2 cup (125 mL) **orange juice** for buttermilk; add grated rind of 1 **orange** to batter along with **raisins**.

For added nutrition use 3/4 cup (175 mL) EACH **whole-wheat flour** and **all-purpose flour**; add 2 tbsp. (30 mL) **bran** and 1 tbsp. (15 mL) **ground flax**.

Cook's Tips

If you don't have buttermilk, make **SOUR MILK** – put 1 tsp. (5 mL) **lemon juice or white vinegar** in a liquid measuring cup, and fill to 1/2 cup (125 mL) mark with **milk**. Let stand 10 minutes to sour. Another good substitution is 1/4 cup (60 mL) plain **yogurt** mixed with 1/4 cup (60 mL) **water**.

Cover the remaining pumpkin and store for up to 3 days in the fridge or up to a month in the freezer. Make more muffins or the Creamy Pumpkin Soup on page 56.

Orange Pecan Bread

Great flavor and texture – try it plain or toasted – with butter or cream cheese.

1	orange, juice of, to make 1/2 cup (125 mL), and grated rind	1
1 1/2 cups	unbleached all-purpose flour	375 mL
2 tsp.	baking powder	10 mL
3/4 cup	sugar	175 mL
1/4 tsp.	salt	1 mL
2 tbsp.	vegetable oil OR melted butter	30 mL
1	egg	1
1/2 cup	chopped pecans (optional)	125 mL

- Preheat oven to 350°F (180°C).

- Lightly grease a 4 x 8" (10 x 20 cm) loaf pan. (I like to put a piece of waxed paper in the bottom – a guarantee that the bread will come out of the pan easily.)

- Scrub orange well with warm water and a little dish soap. Rinse thoroughly and dry. Use a fine grater to grate 2 tsp. (10 mL) of zest (colored part only).

- Squeeze orange and pour juice into a measuring cup. Add enough prepared orange juice or water to make 1/2 cup (125 mL).

- Put flour, baking powder, sugar and salt into a medium bowl. Combine with a fork.

- Combine grated zest, juice, oil and egg in a small bowl. Beat well with a fork or whisk.

- Add orange mixture to flour mixture. Add pecans; **stir until just combined**.

- Scrape batter into prepared pan. Bake for 45-50 minutes, or until a toothpick inserted in the center of the loaf comes out clean.

- Cool in the pan for 10 minutes.

- Run a knife around the inside edge of the pan to loosen bread. Turn out and peel off waxed paper. Cool completely before slicing or storing.

Variations

Add 1/2 cup (125 mL) **raisins**, dried **cranberries or blueberries or** chopped **dates** to the flour mixture – instead of or in addition to the pecans.

For added nutrition use 3/4 cup (175 mL) EACH **whole-wheat flour** and **all-purpose flour**; add 2 tbsp. (30 mL) **bran** and 1 tbsp. (15 mL) **ground flax**.

Cook's Tips

After **zesting orange**, microwave on HIGH for 30 seconds. It will yield more juice.

This bread freezes well – wrap tightly in plastic wrap, then seal in a plastic freezer bag.

B R E A K F A S T S
– A L L D A Y

*N*ever skip breakfast, it is your jump-start for the day. Think whole-grain cereals and breads, fruit or juice and milk or yogurt.

Look in this book for muffins, quick bread recipes and all-day breakfast choices such as omelettes, frittatas and quiches.

Very Veggie – this chapter is loaded with vegetarian choices.

BREAKFAST AT WORK

No time for breakfast! Try packing a breakfast to eat at work. Have a glass of juice or a piece of fruit at home and pack some good things for later.

Try

- **Cottage cheese** and **fruit**
- **Whole-wheat bread**, toasted, with **peanut butter** and a glass of **orange juice**
- **Whole-grain bagel** with **cream cheese or hummus**
- **English muffins** spread with **cream cheese** and **jam**, a glass of **milk** and an **apple** or **orange**
- **Muffin, Cheddar cheese** and a **banana or apple**

For an almost-instant breakfast try

- **Muffin** with a serving of **yogurt, fruit** and **milk**.
- A **fruit smoothie** with 1 or 2 pieces of toast.
- A bowl of **dry cereal** with **milk**, sliced **banana** and **whole-grain toast** – skip the butter in favor of honey.
- A bowl of **fruit** and **yogurt** with a **granola** topping.
- **Whole-wheat bagel**, with low-fat **cream cheese** or **peanut butter**, an **orange** and a glass of **milk**.
- **Whole-grain toast**, with **peanut butter or cheese**, and a glass of **100% fruit juice**.
- Microwaved cooked **cereal** with **blueberries** (still frozen), **milk** and a little **brown sugar**.
- Low-fat **cottage cheese** with **fruit** and **whole-grain toast** or a sprinkle of **granola**.
- Leftover **pizza or** leftover **apple crisp** – well, once in a while.
- **Muesli** with **milk** and a glass of **100% fruit juice**.

Honeyed Orange and Yogurt in a Glass

1 cup	non-fat plain OR vanilla yogurt	250 mL
2 tbsp.	wheat germ OR All-Bran	30 mL
2 tbsp.	frozen orange juice concentrate	30 mL
2 tsp.	honey OR brown sugar	10 mL

• Place all ingredients in a tall glass or small bowl. Whisk until well blended.

SMOOTHIES – Infinite Variety

If you have a blender, your imagination is the only limit to the range of delicious, healthy breakfast or dessert smoothies you can create.

Peach Smoothie

1 cup	skim milk	250 mL
1/2 cup	yogurt OR soft tofu	125 mL
1/2 cup	sliced peaches, fresh, frozen or canned	125 mL
2-3	ice cubes	2-3

• Place all ingredients in a blender and cover. Blend until smooth.

Variations

Experiment – add your favorite flavorings, e.g., **cinnamon**, **almond**, **nutmeg**, **vanilla**, etc. To sweeten, add **honey or maple syrup** to taste.

Fruit Combos to try:

- **Peach Blueberry**
- **Blueberry Mango**
- **Banana Orange**

- **Blueberry Banana**
- **Mango Strawberry**
- **Banana Nectarine**

- **Banana Strawberry**
- **Mango Raspberry**
- **Kiwi Peach**

- **Strawberry Peach**
- **Nectarine Strawberry**
- **Pineapple Orange**

- **Peach Raspberry**
- **Nectarine Blueberry**
- **Pineapple Mango**

Cook's Tips

Try **frozen mixed berries** or **frozen sliced fruit** combinations for quick smoothies – no washing, peeling or slicing fruit, and no need to add ice cubes.

Single servings of **canned fruits** can be part of your smoothie.

For a nutritional boost, add a 1 1/4 oz. (38 g) pouch of **vanilla instant breakfast mix.**

GRANOLA

There are hundreds of recipes for granola. Granola is a mixture of barely cooked seeds, nuts and grains with a little sweetening. Easy to make, it stores well. Granola is good as a cereal, combined with other cereals, eaten as a snack and as a topping on ice cream or yogurt and fruit. A bulk food store or the bulk bins in supermarkets are the best places to buy the ingredients.

Crunchy Granola

Add or delete the items you like or dislike. The bulk of the cereal will be rolled oats or quick-cooking rolled oats.

4 cups	quick-cooking oats	1 L
1 cup	sliced almonds	250 mL
1/2 cup	sunflower seeds	125 mL
1/4 tsp.	cinnamon OR nutmeg	1 mL
2 tbsp.	vegetable oil	30 mL
1/3 cup	honey	75 mL
1 1/3 cups	mixed dried fruit – raisins, cranberries, blueberries, chopped dates and apricots, choose what you like	325 mL

- Preheat oven to 300°F (150°C).

- In a large bowl, combine oats, almonds, seeds and cinnamon.

- In a small pot, heat oil and honey, stir until combined. Pour over the dry ingredients, covering as much as possible. Toss and stir with 2 spoons.

- Spread mixture on a large, lightly oiled, 1 x 10 x 15" (2.5 x 25 x 38 cm) rimmed pan or 2 pizza pans or a pizza pan and a 2 x 9 x 13" (5 x 23 x 33 cm) pan.

- Bake for 40 minutes, stirring every 10 minutes.

- Allow to cool completely. Add dried fruits. Mix well. Store in self-sealing bags.

Variations

LOW-FAT GRANOLA – Replace oil with **orange or apple juice concentrate or applesauce.** Bake at 275°F (135°C) for 1 hour, stirring every 15 minutes.

Replace 1 cup (250 mL) of oats with 1/2 cup (125 mL) EACH **wheat bran** and **wheat germ**.

Add **pumpkin seeds**, **pecans or walnuts**.

Add 1 tsp. (5 mL) **vanilla or almond extract**.

Replace honey with **maple syrup**.

Cook's Tips

ON-THE-GO SNACK MIX – Combine **whole-wheat cereal squares** with trail mix and quartered dried **apricots** or **dates**. Store in a resealable plastic bag. Transfer to snack bags as needed. Great with a glass of milk or juice.

OATMEAL

It is best to buy oatmeal at natural foods or health foods stores. You can buy a small amount and the oatmeal will be fresher and, maybe, cheaper. You can cook a small amount in a small pot or a microwave. Add a few blueberries, fresh or frozen, and eat with milk and a little brown sugar.

1 cup	water	250 mL
¹/₃ cup	rolled oats	75 mL
pinch	salt	pinch

- Combine water, rolled oats and salt in a small saucepan.

- Stir and heat over high heat until oatmeal boils. Reduce heat to low. Cook and stir until water is absorbed, 3-5 minutes.

In the Microwave

1 cup	water	250 mL
¹/₃ cup	rolled oats	75 mL
pinch	salt	pinch

- Combine water, oats and salt in a large cereal bowl. Cover and microwave on high for 90 seconds. Stir and let stand until oatmeal thickens and cooks a little.

Nutrition Note

Fiber is essential to a healthy diet. Besides hastening the elimination process, adding fiber to our diets can lower the risk of heart disease (by having a positive effect on cholesterol); colon, stomach, breast, uterine and ovarian cancers; type 2 diabetes (by helping to regulate or reduce blood sugar levels). **Soluble fiber**, from **oats**, **barley**, **beans**, **brown rice**, **oat bran**, **nuts**, **apples** and **other fruits** and **vegetables**, helps to lower cholesterol. **Insoluble fiber** (roughage), from **whole grains**, **wheat bran**, **nuts**, **beans** and **fruits** and **vegetables**, helps with digestion and elimination, and reduces the toxic effects of some bile acids. It also helps with weight loss.

These fruits contain more than 4 grams of fiber in each serving; **dried apricots**, **raisins**, **cranberries**, **oranges**, **apples**, **pears** and **blueberries**.

Vegetables high in fiber are **peas, carrots, corn, sweet potato, baked potato with skin, green beans, broccoli** and **asparagus**.

Good choices in pulses are **kidney, garbanzo** and **pinto beans**, also **lentils**.

Good sources for grains with loads of fiber are **oat bran** and **barley, 100% whole-grain bread, all-bran** and **whole-wheat cereal**.

Cook's Tip

When you add fruit to your cereal you add vitamins and fiber. Try sliced **bananas, peaches, oranges** or **strawberries** or try **raspberries, raisins** or dried **cranberries**. If you don't have fresh fruit, use frozen.

PANCAKES

One of the good things about pancakes is the wide variety of additions and toppings. Also, think of them for lunch or a late meal when nothing else appeals.

1 cup	unbleached all-purpose flour OR	250 mL
	use 1/2 whole-wheat and 1/2 all-purpose flour	
2 tsp.	baking powder	10 mL
pinch	salt	pinch
1 tbsp.	sugar	15 mL
1 1/4 cups	milk, any kind	300 mL
1	egg	1
2 tbsp.	vegetable oil OR melted butter OR margarine	30 mL

- Combine flour, baking powder, salt and sugar in a medium-sized mixing bowl.

- In a small bowl or in a 2-cup (500 mL) measure, whisk together milk, egg and oil.

- Add milk mixture to flour mixture. Mix gently until just combined (a few lumps are OK).

- Heat a non-stick pan over medium heat; spray with vegetable oil. Use a 1/3 cup (75 mL) measure to drop pancake batter on the hot pan. Turn once. The pancakes are ready to turn when the edges look brown and the batter is bubbly and beginning to set. Repeat with remaining batter. There is no need to add more oil to the pan.

Makes 6 pancakes

GO WITHS – Serve pancakes, all kinds, with **maple syrup** – and **butter** if you like. For a treat, with the sweet pancakes, try sliced **strawberries or peaches** and a spoonful of **sour cream or whipped cream**.

Variations

For thinner, more **crêpe-like pancakes**, increase the amount of **milk**. Add another 1/4 cup (60 mL) or experiment until the pancakes are just the way you like them.

BLUEBERRY PANCAKES – Add 1/2 cup (125 mL) fresh or frozen **blueberries** to the batter.

STRAWBERRY OR RASPBERRY PANCAKES – Add 1/2 cup (125 mL) sliced **strawberries or** whole **raspberries** to the batter.

BANANA PANCAKES – Add 3 or 4 thin **banana** slices to the pancake on the pan. Turn the pancake and continue cooking. You may have to wipe out the pan and re-oil after cooking 2 or 3 pancakes as the banana sticks a bit.

APPLE PANCAKES – Add 1/2 cup (125 mL) chopped **apple** to the batter.

SAVORY CORN PANCAKES – Add 1/2 cup (125 mL) **corn niblets** to the batter. These are great with pork sausages or bacon.

French Toast

A crispy, golden crust and a tender melting center – so easy and so good.

1	large egg	1
1/4 cup	milk	60 mL
1/2 tsp.	sugar	2 mL
1/4 tsp.	vanilla	1 mL
3 slices	bread (French bread is best)	3 slices

- In a small bowl or cup, using a fork or a whisk, combine egg, milk, sugar and vanilla. Pour into a flat bowl or a deep plate.

- Spray a small non-stick pan with vegetable oil or coat with butter. Heat over medium heat.

- Dip bread slices in the egg mixture. Turn to coat second side.

- Cook bread, 1 or 2 slices at a time, until golden brown. Turn once.

GO WITHS – **maple syrup** and **sour cream**; with a sprinkle of **cinnamon**, **applesauce** and **sour cream**; with **blueberry sauce** and **whipped cream**; with **jam** and **icing (confectioner's) sugar**, or just with a sprinkle of **brown sugar**.

Sugary Apple Topping

Delicious on french toast, pancakes or even ice cream.

1/4 cup	butter OR margarine	60 mL
2	apples, cored and sliced	2
1/4 cup	packed brown sugar	60 mL
1/4 cup	chopped nuts	60 mL
2 tbsp.	water	30 mL

In a skillet, melt butter. Add apples and cook, stirring occasionally, until tender. Stir in brown sugar, nuts and water; heat through. Serve warm.

Variations

Substitute **peaches, nectarines or mangoes** for the apples.

Easy Maple Syrup

When your budget won't stretch to buy the real thing, this is an inexpensive substitute.

2 cups	sugar	500 mL
1 cup	water	250 mL
1/2 tsp.	maple extract	2 mL

In a small saucepan, bring sugar and water to a boil. Remove from heat. Stir in maple extract.

EGGS AND CHEESE

Eggs are an excellent protein source, which makes them a good meat substitute with the convenience of an easily stored, almost perfect package provided by nature. They can be a meal in an omelette or quiche, become a Denver sandwich or a frittata, or an add-to in a salad or a curry. There are endless ways to cook and combine them.

Cheese, too, provides a nutritious alternative to meat. Make a meal of a Cheese Quesadilla, page 104, or a Monte Cristo, page 35. You can add cheese to everything. Well, almost everything. Add it to salads, wraps, egg dishes, pastas and to chili, as a topping.

Scrambled Eggs

All-Day Breakfast is a perfect name for these versatile, satisfying eggs.

- Spray a small non-stick pan with vegetable oil. Heat on medium.

- In a cup or a small bowl, using a fork or a small whisk to mix, combine **2 eggs**, **2 tbsp. (30 mL) of milk or water** and a **pinch of salt**. Pour into pan.

- With a fork or wooden spoon, push eggs, as they set, into pan center. Fold eggs gently as they thicken. Cook and stir until eggs are set but still moist and shiny looking, 3-4 minutes. Sprinkle with black pepper.

GO WITHS – Serve on toast with sliced tomatoes on the side.

Variations

Add a slice of **low-fat cheese** to the eggs on the plate and/or sprinkle with a few **bacon bits**, or serve with **mild to hot salsa**.

Per egg, stir in 1 tbsp. (15 mL) of 1 of the following:
  - sautéed sliced **mushrooms**
  - sautéed **red, yellow or green peppers**
  - sautéed **asparagus tips**
  - sautéed **zucchini**
  - sautéed **green or white onions**
  - roasted **red peppers**
  - **smoked salmon**
  - grated **Cheddar, Swiss or Parmesan cheese**
  - chopped herbs – **chives, dill or parsley** – 1 tbsp. (15 mL) fresh, or 1 tsp. (5 mL) dried

Nutrition Note

Eggs provide high-density nutrition. One large egg contains only 70 calories, 6 g of protein and only 5 g of fat (including only 1.5 g saturated fat and NO trans fats). The yolk provides 11 essential vitamins and minerals. Eggs are also an excellent source of choline, which plays an important role in memory and brain development, and of lutein and zeaxanthin, antioxidants which contribute to healthy eyes and protecting eyes from ultraviolet rays. (CEMA. *Omelettes – Perfect Anytime*, Centax Books, Regina 2003)

Tomato Cheese Omelet

Very quick and perfect for breakfast, lunch or dinner.

2	eggs	2
2 tbsp.	water	30 mL
	salt and pepper to taste	
1 tsp.	vegetable oil OR butter	5 mL
1	tomato, chopped (use 2 or 3 Romas if you wish)	1
1 cup	shredded Cheddar OR mozzarella cheese	250 mL

- Whisk eggs with water, salt and pepper in a small bowl.

- In a large, non-stick skillet, heat oil over medium heat. Tip pan to evenly coat the bottom. Add eggs to pan. Reduce heat a little. Cook eggs until beginning to set. Gently lift eggs at the edges of the pan and tilt pan so that uncooked egg runs under the omelette.

- When egg is almost set, sprinkle half of the omelette with tomatoes and cheese. With a large spatula, fold the other half of the omelette over the tomatoes and cheese. Cook for about 2 minutes, until cheese is melted and tomato is warmed. Loosen edges of omelette and slide onto a plate.

Serves 1 – 3 eggs will serve 2. Additional ingredients remain the same.

GO WITHS – A **green salad** and **toast**.

Variations

Try chopped **ham** and grated **cheese**; crumbled crisp **bacon**; sautéed **mushrooms**; sautéed **green** and **red peppers**; a spoonful of **salsa**, anything goes.

MEDITERRANEAN OMELET – Substitute 2 tbsp. (30 mL) crumbled **feta** for the Cheddar cheese and 1 tbsp. (15 mL) slivered **sun-dried tomatoes** (in oil) for the tomato. Also add 1 tsp. (5 mL) of **capers**.

SEAFOOD OMELET – Top the basic omelet (without the tomato and cheese) with sautéed **green onions**, **scallops and/or shrimp**. Optional additions are sautéed **peppers**, **mushrooms** and **salsa**.

Cook's Tips

If you prefer your omelets to be set a bit more than a traditional omelet, without browning the bottom too much, use an ovenproof skillet and place the omelet under a preheated broiler for a few seconds, after the fillings are added, to set the surface of the omelet.

To make perfect omelets, stick to the 3-egg size and make as many as you need.

To make a larger omelet, increase the eggs to 6, the water to $1/4$ cup (60 mL) and cooking time as needed. Use a larger pan if you have it.

For a classy presentation, sprinkle the folded omelet with grated cheese; broil until cheese is melted and lightly browned.

Vegetable Frittata

A frittata is a little more substantial than an omelette, the eggs are finished in the oven or covered; no folding is needed.

2 tsp.	vegetable oil	10 mL
1/2-1 cup	mixed, chopped vegetables – red or green pepper, broccoli, mushrooms, zucchini, tomatoes, cooked potato, green onion	125-250 mL
	salt and pepper to taste	
2	eggs	2
1/2 cup	grated mozzarella OR Cheddar cheese	125 mL
	sprinkle of dried basil OR Italian seasoning	

- Heat oil in a small or medium-sized non-stick skillet over medium-high heat. Tip pan to evenly coat the bottom.

- Add vegetables of your choice. Cook and stir until tender, about 3 minutes. Sprinkle with salt and pepper.

- Whisk eggs, cheese and basil in a small bowl and pour over vegetable mixture. Stir.

- Cook, lifting edges gently with a spatula so that egg mixture combines with veggies and flows to the bottom of the pan. Turn the broiler on about now.

- Continue to cook until the edges are set and the bottom is starting to brown (lift with a spatula to look), about 3 minutes.

- Wrap pan handle with foil if it is not ovenproof. Place the frittata under the broiler until the top is set and lightly browned, about 2 minutes.

- Use a knife or spatula to loosen frittata at the edges. Slide onto a plate or cut in half and serve from the pan.

Variations

Any vegetables are good – be sure to also try **asparagus**. I like to sprinkle extra **cheese** on top just before browning in the oven.

MEDITERRANEAN FRITTATA – add chopped **Greek or Italian olives** and substitute **feta** for the other cheeses.

Cook's Tip

Use eggs that are at least 1 week old for hard-boiled eggs. They will be easier to peel.

Mexican Frittata

Good for a quick meal, lunch, supper or brunch Serve with whole-grain toast.

2 tsp.	butter OR vegetable oil	10 mL
1/2	green OR red pepper, diced	1/2
1/2	small onion, diced	1/2
1	tomato, diced	1
2-3 tbsp.	frozen corn kernels	30-45 mL
	salt and pepper to taste	
2	eggs, beaten (use a fork and beat them in a cup)	2
1 or 2	low-fat cheese slices OR a sprinkle of grated cheese	1 or 2

- Heat butter or oil in a medium-sized non-stick skillet over medium heat.

- Add green pepper and onion. Cook and stir until onion becomes translucent and begins to brown at the edges. Add tomato, corn, salt and pepper. Cook and stir until heated through.

- Pour in eggs and cook until set. Stir so that uncooked egg can flow to the bottom.

- Place cheese slices on top of almost cooked eggs. Cover with a pot lid for 1-2 minutes, to finish the cooking and melt cheese OR use an ovenproof skillet and place under a preheated broiler for a few seconds to set top and melt cheese.

Variations

TUNA AND MUSHROOM FRITTATA – Omit corn, sauté 2 sliced **mushrooms** with **onion** and **peppers**. Stir in 3-4 tbsp. (45-60 mL) flaked **tuna**; pour in eggs and cook as above.

POTATO MUSHROOM FRITTATA – Omit tomato and corn, sauté 1 sliced **cooked potato**, 2 chopped **mushrooms** with **peppers**. Pour in eggs; add cheese; cover and cook for 6-7 minutes, until set. Cut in wedges and serve with salsa.

Cook's Tip

Moldy cheese is not a problem. Small amounts of mold can be cut off and the cheese used as you need it. I find it helpful to keep small amounts of cheese in the fridge and the remainder in a resealable bag in the freezer.

Crustless Cheddar Quiche

Ready for the oven in less than 10 minutes and cooked in 30. Crustless means less fat and less time – this Cheddar quiche is loaded with good food value.

2	eggs	2
1 cup	milk or 1% evaporated milk	250 mL
2 tbsp.	all-purpose flour	30 mL
1/2 tsp.	baking powder	2 mL
	salt and pepper to taste	
1/8 tsp.	ground nutmeg	0.5 mL
1/2-1 cup	cooked broccoli florets	125-250 mL
1/2 cup	grated Cheddar cheese	125 mL
1	green onion, chopped (optional)	1

- Preheat oven to 350°F (180° C).

- Oil a 6" (15 cm) casserole, about 3-cup (750 mL) size.

- Combine eggs and milk in a bowl; whisk well. Whisk in flour, baking powder, salt, pepper, and nutmeg.

- Pour egg mixture into prepared pan. Distribute cheese evenly over egg mixture; add onion if using.

- Bake for 30 minutes, or until set at the edges but still jiggly in the middle.

GO WITHS – FOR BREAKFAST, serve with **whole-wheat toast or bran muffins**. FOR LUNCH OR SUPPER, serve with an **orange and romaine salad or sliced tomatoes**.

Eggs in a Nest

	butter OR margarine	
2 slices	bread	2 slices
2	eggs	2
	salt and pepper to taste	

- Spread butter on bread. Cut a circle from the center of each bread slice.

- Melt a little butter in a medium skillet over medium-low heat. Place bread and circles in pan. Crack 1 egg into each circle. Cook until bread is lightly browned and egg almost set. Turn to cook other side. Sprinkle with salt and pepper.

Cook's Tip

1% evaporated milk is a good low-fat substitute for cream in quiche, sauces and baking. It gives a nutritional boost, too. Evaporated skim milk has almost no fat. It adds creaminess to sauces and soups and is convenient to have on hand.

S U P E R - Q U I C K
M E A L S

Here is a quick reference for single-serving meals, the kind that you need when you have only a few minutes in the kitchen. With a glass of skim milk and a serving of fruit, each meal idea becomes a complete meal and a good part of your daily nutritional needs. Not gourmet fare or Sunday dinner specials, these are good food choices to replace "fast food".

- Super-Quick Savory Breads, page 21
- Super-Quick Meal Choices, page 38
- Super-Quick Wraps or Roll-Ups, page 40
- Super-Quick Soups, pages 53, 54
- Super-Quick Meal Salads, page 60
- Super-Quick Single-Serving Pasta, Potato, Rice and Couscous Essentials, page 76
- Super-Quick Rice Dishes, page 84
- Super-Quick Pasta Sauces, pages 90, 91
- Super-Quick Pizzas, page 100
- Super-Quick Quesadillas, page 104
- Super-Quick Chicken, page 116
- Super-Quick Ground Meat Specials, page 124
- Super-Quick Burgers, page 133
- Stir-Fry "Meals-In-Minutes", page 139

A meal earns the title Super-Quick when it can be made in less than 15 minutes and prepared from items usually on hand in the cupboard, fridge or freezer. Most of the recipes in this book are for single servings. The ingredients are always available where you shop and they are easy to transport and to store.

This book, with its super-quick recipes, is for all those I talked to who said, "I want recipes for 1 person, 1 serving. I don't want to divide the recipe and I don't want to store the leftover food."

Very Veggie – the Super-Quick recipe options are loaded with vegetarian choices.

SUPER-QUICK SALAD MEALS

A green salad becomes a dinner salad when you top it with sliced tomatoes, a few frozen corn kernels thawed, a bit of green onion or cucumber, your favorite dressing, and 1 or 2 of the following:

- Strips of sliced cooked **chicken breast**
- Strips of diced deli **ham**, **turkey**, **roast beef or** barbecued **steak**
- Chunked, drained canned **tuna or salmon**
- Chopped **hard-boiled egg**, cubed **Cheddar cheese**, **chickpeas or kidney beans**
- **Greek olives** and cubed **feta cheese**

SUPER-QUICK MEAL CHOICES

Here are some useful ideas for preparing the good food you have stored in your cupboards and fridge. Quickly prepared, they are satisfying, more nutritious and less expensive than stopping for fast food – probably quicker too. Add milk and fruit to each meal.

- **Grilled cheese sandwich** with a serving of **tomato soup or** canned **pineapple**
- **Tuna or Shrimp Melt**, page 44, with sliced **tomatoes**
- **Toasted sardine sandwich** with **ketchup** and a **green salad**
- **Ham, tomato and cheese melt** with a dish of **fruit**
- **Cheese Quesadilla**, page 104, with **salsa** and **sour cream**, an **apple** for dessert
- A **Chicken or Ham Quesadilla**, page 104
- A **poached egg** with canned **beans in tomato sauce** and **whole-wheat toast**
- **Scrambled eggs** with grated **cheese** and **spicy salsa**, **fruit** and **cookies** for dessert
- A **cheese omelette** with **toast** and canned **peaches** or **pears**
- Single-serving **vegetable soup** with a **toasted peanut butter sandwich** and a dish of **applesauce**
- **Salmon salad sandwich** with a **tomato** and **lettuce salad**
- Frozen purchased **burritos** heated with a little **tomato sauce** and **Cheddar cheese**, an **orange**, too
- A **baked potato** topped with **cheese** and **broccoli** with a small **salad** or **fruit**
- A **baked potato** topped with canned **chili** and grated **cheese**, a **salad** or **fruit**
- Sautéed **perogies** with **onions** and **sour cream**, with a **green salad**
- **Cottage cheese** with canned **pineapple** and **whole-wheat toast**
- A **tortilla pizza** made with **tomato sauce**, slivered **vegetables** and grated **cheese**
- Your favorite **pasta** topped with a 1 or 2 spoonfuls of commercial **pesto sauce**, with a **tomato and feta salad**, **fruit** and **cookies** for dessert

DELI MEALS

Recently, when I was travelling long miles through Manitoba and northern Ontario, I stopped late – tired and hungry. I was longing for comfort food to soothe the gnawing hunger in my stomach. I sat alone in an empty restaurant, waited a long time to be served my meal of grilled sirloin and baked potato. My stomach was soothed but I wasn't. The next night, after another long day, I stopped at a deli. I bought a roasted chicken quarter, lightly dressed Greek salad and a crusty roll, and took them back to the hotel room. The supermarket deli supplied the plate and plastic knife and fork. I dined well and deliciously and at half the cost, too. Happy with my experience, I returned to the deli at the supermarket and I had a long chat with the helpful clerk. I learned a lot. Many delis now feature single servings of salads, ribs, chicken and a range of starters. Make them part of your weekly meal planning. Believe me, they taste even better when eaten at home.

SANDWICHES

Choose your favorite bread – **pumpernickel, whole-grain**, a **hamburger bun** or **Kaiser roll**, or a split **pita bread**. Choose a few ingredients from the fridge or cupboard and quickly make a sandwich.

SANDWICH FILLING CHOICES

- Combine a 3½ oz. (106 g) can of **salmon, tuna or shrimp**, drained, with a little **mayo, yogurt or creamy salad dressing**. Add a little chopped **celery or cucumber** for crunch. Try a pinch of **curry powder** with the shrimp or tuna for a subtle flavor enhancement.

- Combine chopped leftover deli **chicken** with a little **mayo or creamy salad dressing** and a little chopped **cucumber, celery or red bell pepper**. No deli chicken? Try 1-2 chopped **hard-boiled eggs**.

- Stack sliced **deli or home-cooked meats** with sliced **tomatoes, pickles, cheese, mayo or creamy dressing** and **lettuce**. In a bun it's a sub or hero.

- Sliced **meatloaf** with **chutney** on **whole-grain bread** is one of my favorite sandwiches.

- HOAGIE – Slice a crusty **Italian or French roll** horizontally. Sprinkle both halves with **olive oil**. Top one half with shredded **lettuce, Italian ham or salami or roast beef or tuna salad or deli chicken or turkey breast**. Add your choice of – sliced **onions,** **tomatoes,** sautéed **mushrooms, hot or sweet peppers or roasted red peppers**. Top with slices of **provolone cheese** and the other half of the roll.

- GREEK HOAGIE – Spread **crusty rolls** with **garlic olive oil or garlic mayo**. Top with sliced grilled **chicken,** crumbled **feta**, sliced **Greek olives**, sliced **onions** and **tomatoes** and **lettuce**.

Some days a soup and sandwich, a salad and sandwich or just a sandwich may be exactly what you want for a quick evening meal – don't limit your options by relegating sandwiches to the lunch menu.

Very Veggie – this chapter is loaded with vegetarian choices.

SUPER-QUICK WRAPS OR ROLL-UPS

Call them what you like. Here is a basic recipe. Be creative and design your own.

When packed for lunch or stored in the fridge for later, I like to **heat wraps for 30 seconds on HIGH in the microwave to improve the flavor and texture of the tortilla.**

Amounts for wraps don't need to be exact. You will need about 4 oz. (115 g) of **ham or roast beef or turkey**, 3 **cheese slices or** about 4 oz. (115 g) of **cheese** for each wrap. It's a guessing game.

- Soften 4 oz. (125 g) of **cream cheese** or use the spreadable variety.
- Add 1 tsp. (5 mL) **Dijon mustard** and a little chopped **onion, red or green peppers.**
- Spread on 2 large **flour tortillas.**
- Sprinkle with grated **Swiss** or **Cheddar cheese** – be sure to leave a 1" (2.5 cm) space on the upper edge of the tortilla, so it will seal when wrapped.
- Cover thinly with chopped **lettuce** and thinly sliced good-quality deli **ham**, about 4 oz. (115 g) for each tortilla.
- Gently, but firmly roll up the tortilla. Cut in 2 or 3 pieces and serve immediately OR wrap in plastic wrap and keep in the fridge till needed.

Variations

For excellent **snacks and starters**, cut wraps in 1" (25. cm) diagonal slices.

VEGGIE WRAP – Omit meat and sprinkle finely chopped **broccoli, mushrooms, cucumber, tomato, celery** and/or **hot pickled peppers** over the **cheese.**

SEAFOOD WRAP – Omit meat and mustard and add drained canned **shrimp or crab, tuna, canned or smoked salmon**. Sprinkle with **lemon juice** if you have it.

CURRIED CHICKEN WRAP – Use the filling from the **Pita Pockets** on page 41.

CHILI WRAP – Use leftover **chili** as a wrap filling. Add lettuce if you have it.

Chicken Bunwiches

Make a salad with prewashed greens, orange slices and a light creamy or vinaigrette dressing and your meal is ready.

1	boneless, skinless chicken breast	1
1 tsp.	vegetable oil	5 mL
	salt and pepper OR seasoning salt	
1	hamburger bun OR crusty roll	1
	butter OR margarine OR mustard mayonnaise	
	lettuce, tomato and/or cucumber slices	

Chicken Bunwiches   *continued*

- Using a meat mallet or the heel of your hand, flatten the chicken breast between 2 pieces of plastic wrap or in a plastic bag. Discard wrap or bag.

- Brush chicken with oil; sprinkle with salt and pepper or seasoning salt. Heat an oiled non-stick skillet over medium-high heat. Place chicken in skillet and cook, turning once, until no longer pink, about 8 minutes. Reduce heat if pan gets too hot.

- Transfer chicken to a plate and let cool slightly. Serve on a heated bun spread with butter or mayonnaise. If the chicken breast is too thick, slice in half horizontally.

- Top chicken with lettuce, tomato and cucumber.

Variations

Top with crumbled **blue cheese** or **feta cheese** if you prefer.

Add **mango** or **cranberry chutney** for a completely different flavor version.

Curried Chicken Pita Pockets

Make these with leftover chicken or turkey or one of those extra chicken breasts you cooked.

1	cooked chicken breast (about 8 oz./250 g), cut in 1/2″ (1.3 cm) pieces	1
1/4 cup	mayonnaise OR a mixture of mayonnaise and yogurt	60 mL
2 tsp.	curry powder	10 mL
1/2 cup	halved green grapes	125 mL
1/4 cup	chopped peanuts OR cashews	60 mL
	salt to taste	
2, 6″	pita pockets OR 4, 3″ (8 cm) pitas*	2, 15 cm
4	lettuce leaves	4
	mango chutney (optional)	

- In a small bowl, gently combine chicken, mayonnaise, curry powder, grapes, nuts and salt.

- Heat pita pockets for a few seconds in a microwave or a minute or so in a toaster oven to make them easier to handle. Cut in half, making 4 pockets. Open gently.

- Put lettuce in each pocket, add chicken mixture and a little chutney.

Cook's Tip

MINI POCKETS filled with **curried chicken** are an easy-to-fix starter and great to take to a party. Cut in half and stuff. They are a bit fiddly to make but worth it. Tuck a small piece of **lettuce or parsley** into each pocket for eye appeal. Remember to keep pockets cool when you transport them and to discard the leftovers.

Denver Sandwich

Sometimes called a Western, this old standby is always satisfying.

1 tsp.	vegetable oil OR butter	5 mL
1	green onion, sliced	1
1	slice cooked ham, diced	1
2	eggs	2
	sprinkle of salt and pepper	
2	slices buttered toast	2

- Heat a little oil in a small non-stick pan over medium heat. Add onion and ham. Cook and stir until onion softens and ham is heated through.
- Break eggs into a cup and whisk with a fork. Pour over ham and onion.
- Use a spatula to lift egg edges, to allow uncooked egg to flow under. Sprinkle with salt and pepper. Continue until egg is set. Place eggs between toast slices.

Variations

BACON DENVER – Use chopped sliced **bacon** instead of ham. Vary the vegetables too, add **red or green pepper** and **mushrooms or** top the egg with **cheese** and **tomato** slices.

REUBEN DENVER – Use 2 thin slices of diced **corned beef** instead of the ham. Add a slice of **Swiss cheese** and some **Dijon mustard**.

GRILLED SANDWICHES

Put filling between 2 slices of **bread**; spread **butter** on outside of **bread**. Cook in a non-stick pan over medium heat until golden brown, 2-3 minutes on each side.

Filling Options

- Sliced **cheese or cheese and ham** with **mustard** – try **Cheddar, Swiss or mozzarella**. Add a **tomato** slice if you like.
- **Swiss cheese**, sliced **corned beef** and sliced **dill pickles**
- Leftover sautéed or salad **vegetables** with sliced **Cheddar cheese, pesto or mayo**

Monte Cristo

A classic combo – good with fruit salad or a dish of applesauce.

	butter and mustard	
4 slices	bread	4 slices
4 slices	Swiss cheese	4 slices
2 slices	cooked ham	2 slices
1	egg, beaten	1
2 tbsp.	milk	30 mL

- Spread 2 slices of bread with butter and mustard. Place a slice of Swiss cheese on each. Top with a slice of ham. Top with remaining slices of bread.
- Beat egg and milk together. Dip sandwiches in egg mixture.
- Brown sandwiches on both sides in lightly oiled or buttered pan.

GRILLED SANDWICHES   *continued*

Grilled Veggie Sandwich

For a grilled veggie sandwich sauté about 1 cup (250 mL) of some of the following: sliced **mushrooms, onions, green or red peppers** or sliced **broccoli**. Place on **bread**, spread with **mayo or mustard**, cover with grated **Cheddar or mozzarella cheese** and thin slices of **tomato**. Top with a second slice of **bread**. Spread outside of both slices lightly with **butter or margarine** and cook on both sides in a non-stick pan until heated through and cheese is melted.

Grilled Club Sandwiches – Call it a Panini

I recently purchased a super sandwich. It was full of good things and cooked top and bottom in a grill. Cooking 1 side at a time on a non-stick pan gives the same delicious results.

Choose extra-thick **multi-grain bread**, a small **foccacia**, cut in half horizontally, **or** 2 **hamburger buns**; make a "Dagwood"; grill and serve.

- Spray a little **olive oil** on the bottom slice of **bread**. Add thin slices of good-quality **deli meat**, sliced **cheese** and sliced **tomato or cucumber**. Sprinkle with a little **balsamic vinegar or pickle juice** (from the jar). Add **salt** and **pepper** to taste, the top slice of **bread**, and press down gently. Cook in a lightly oiled non-stick pan on medium heat until lightly browned. Turn with a spatula or 2 forks and brown the other side.

Club Combos – Try

- **Ham** with sliced **Swiss cheese**, sliced **tomatoes** and a little **mayo**
- **Olive bread** with **ham**, sliced **Swiss cheese, green pepper** and **garlic butter or oil**
- Sliced **turkey or chicken**, a little chopped **onion**, chopped **peanuts or cashews** and **mayo**, mixed with a 1/4 tsp. (1 mL) of **curry powder**
- Leftover deli **chicken** with **chutneys** and sliced **cucumbers**
- VEGGIE SPECIAL GRILLED CLUB SANDWICH – Cover the bottom slice of **bread** with thinly sliced **cheese**, layer with thinly sliced **tomato, cucumber** and **onion**. Add **asparagus**, if you have it. Add a little **mayo**, another slice of **cheese** and the top slice of bread. Grill as above.

Cook's Tip

Grilled sandwiches cook faster and are cheesier when weighted. Put a plate on top of the sandwich and weigh down with a can of tomatoes.

MELTS

Toast 1 side of the **bread**, **bun or English muffin**, turn it over and spread with the filling; top with **cheese** and bake or broil. Now it's a melt. Add a salad or a bowl of fruit and it's a meal. Try:

- **Tomato** and **cheese**, OR **ham**, **tomato** and **cheese**.

- Drained **tuna or shrimp** mixed with a little **mayo**, **yogurt or creamy dressing**. Top with grated **Cheddar or Swiss cheese**.

Variations

PHILADELPHIA CHEESE STEAK – Slice a crusty **Italian or French bread roll** in half lengthwise. Top each half with shredded **roast beef or** very thinly sliced cooked **steak**; top with **provolone cheese**. Broil until cheese is hot and bubbly, about 1 minute.

Substitute shredded grilled **chicken** for roast beef or steak – less authentic – still great!

Tuna Melts

Tuna melts and wraps are easily and quickly made in an oven or toaster oven and can be a quick meal. Make more if you are hungry or serve them with a bowl of soup.

3 oz.	can flaked or solid white tuna, drained	95 g
2 tbsp.	EACH finely chopped celery, green onion, and	30 mL
	mayonnaise OR yogurt	
	salt and pepper to taste	
1	English muffin, split OR 2 thick slices whole-wheat bread	1
¼ cup	grated Cheddar OR Swiss cheese	60 mL

- In a small bowl, combine tuna, celery, onion, mayonnaise, salt and pepper.

- Toast 1 side of muffins or bread under the broiler or in a toaster oven. Turn muffins/bread over and spread with tuna mixture. Top with grated cheese.

- Return to broiler or toaster oven; broil or toast until cheese is heated and bubbly.

Variation

SHRIMP MELT – Substitute shrimp for tuna.

Cheesy Tuna Topper

Dressed-up buns make good eating.

Combine drained canned **tuna** with a little **mayo** to moisten. Add some chopped **green onions** and **pickles**.

- Spread on halved buns. Top with a sprinkle of grated **cheese** or a cheese slice. Broil or toast until bubbly.

S N A C K S &
S T A R T E R S

Roasted Almonds

Serve with a glass of wine, also sprinkle on salads.

1 tsp.	olive oil	5 mL
2 cups	almonds, with or without skins	500 mL
	a sprinkle of salt	

- Heat a non-stick pan over medium-high heat. Add oil and almonds. Stir and cook until heated through and beginning to brown. Sprinkle with salt. Cool and store in an airtight container.

Hummus

Good nutrition and great flavor, also super-quick

In a food processor or blender, place 19 oz. (540 mL) can **chickpeas**, drained; add juice of 1 **lemon**, 2-3 **garlic cloves**, 1/2 tsp. (2 mL) **cumin**, **salt** and **pepper** to taste. Process until smooth. Add 2-3 tbsp. (30-45 mL) chopped **fresh parsley**, if you have it, and 1 tbsp. (15 mL) **tahini (sesame) paste** for a more authentic Middle Eastern flavor. You can also add up to 1/4 cup (60 mL) **olive oil** and a splash of **hot pepper sauce**. Serve with pita bread, Pita Crisps, page 46, or a variety of fresh vegetable dippers.

Yield 2 cups (500 mL)

S uper-quick homemade snacks and starters can be tastier, healthier and less expensive than fat-laden commercial products.

Starters are very versatile – for many people they are the best part of a meal – loaded with flavor and offering lots of variety.

Very Veggie – most of these recipes are vegetarian – so they are perfect for any group of friends. The exceptions are on page 52, some of the wrap fillings and the Turkey Pinwheels.

Cook's Tips

This amount of Hummus is enough for a party. Put out half at a time. Replenish with fridge stock. Discard any hummus left at room temperature.

Hummus leftovers from the fridge can be used as a sandwich spread or veggie dip.

Salsa

There is no need to commit to a large jar of salsa. Make a 1-tomato portion to serve with a quesadilla or fajita.

Coarsely chop 1 ripe **tomato** and 1 **green onion**. Place in a small bowl and add 1 crushed **garlic clove**, 1 tbsp. (15 mL) of **cider or red wine vinegar**, a ¼ tsp. (1 mL) **hot sauce** and a sprinkle of **salt**. Mix well. Add 1-2 tbsp. (15-30 mL) of chopped **fresh cilantro** if you wish.

TORTILLA SNACKS

Spread a few **tortilla chips** on a microwave-safe plate. Top chips with shredded medium **Cheddar cheese**, chopped **red onion** and **green pepper**; add a few chopped **green chilies** if you like. Microwave on HIGH just until the cheese melts, about 20-30 seconds. Serve as finger food with **salsa** and **sour cream**.

Variations

PARMESAN TRIANGLES – Split pita bread rounds in half horizontally. Lightly brush the cut side of each pita **bread** half with melted **butter or olive oil**. Cut each half into 3 wedges. Place on a cookie pan. Sprinkle with grated **Parmesan or Romano cheese**. Bake at 375°F (190°C) for 6-8 minutes, or until crisp. This is a perfect toaster-oven snack.

TOASTED TORTILLAS – Cut **flour tortillas** into 4 quarters, toast in a toaster oven until heated and beginning to brown at edges or bake at 400°F (200°C) for 8-10 minutes. They will crisp as they cool. Cool and store in self-sealing bags (for 1-2 weeks). They are good with dips, spreads or crumbled and sprinkled on soups and salads.

Tortilla Pizza Snack

For a super-quick snack or an accompaniment for soup or salad, top a **tortilla or pita bread** with a little squeeze-bottle **pizza sauce**, a little grated **mozzarella or Cheddar cheese** and toast it in the oven or toaster oven until bubbly. Good Food!

Pita Crisps

Pita crisps for dips and snacks. Tastier than crackers and low in fat.

Preheat oven to 425°F (220°C). Cut pita breads into 8 triangles. Separate each at the fold to make 16 triangles. Arrange rough side up on a cookie sheet and bake for 8-10 minutes, until golden and crisp. Store in a tightly closed container or plastic bag.

Variation

As a special treat, spray with **olive oil** and sprinkle with **herbs** just before baking. I like **Italian herbs or herbes de Provence** – both are available in most supermarkets.

Cook's Tip

Cut pita pockets with kitchen scissors. It's easier.

Mini Pita Pizzas

These are good for a snack or for party fare. These pizzas are mini, therefore, they need mini amounts of topping. Heat the broiler (toaster oven if you are just making a few). Cover mini pitas with a little **tomato sauce** *and a sprinkle of* **basil or pizza seasoning,** *a little grated* **cheese** *and decorate with finely chopped pieces of:*

> **red OR green pepper**
> **Roma tomato**
> **thinly sliced red onion OR mushroom**
> **freshly grated Parmesan cheese**
> **toasted pine nuts and a little bit of feta cheese**

- Broil until bubbly, about 5 minutes.

NOTE – If you use 7" (18 cm) pitas, it is better to split them in half horizontally to form 2 rounds. Bake and cut in quarters to serve.

Layered Chili Dip

Substantial and satisfying, this hot dip is great to share.

4 oz.	cream cheese, softened	125 g
1/4 cup	grated mozzarella OR pizza-blend cheese	60 mL
2 tbsp.	chopped onion	30 mL
8 oz.	canned chili	250 mL
4 1/4 oz.	can chopped green chilies, drained (optional)	114 mL
1/4 cup	grated mozzarella OR pizza-blend cheese	60 mL

- Preheat oven to 350°F (180°C).
- Spread cream cheese over a small casserole top or a flat ovenproof dish, about 7" (18 cm) size.
- Combine cheeses, onion, chili and green chilies, if using. Spread over cream cheese.
- Sprinkle with grated cheese and bake for 10-15 minutes, until hot and bubbly.
- Serve with tortilla chips as dippers.

Makes about 2 cups (500 mL)

Quick Creamy Cucumber Dip

Serve with carrot sticks, broccoli florets, red or green pepper strips, cucumber slices, etc.

Combine equal amounts of plain **fat-free yogurt** with **creamy cucumber salad dressing**. Stir in a pinch of **sugar**, or more, to taste. Try a **creamy ranch dressing** as well.

Smoked Salmon Spread

4 oz.	cream cheese, softened	125 g
1 tbsp.	plain yogurt OR mayonnaise	15 mL
4 oz.	smoked salmon, finely chopped (1/2 cup [125 mL])	125 g
1 tsp.	fresh lemon juice	5 mL
pinch	finely grated lemon zest and freshly ground black pepper	pinch

Flavor Options
1-2 tbsp. (15-30 mL) finely chopped onion
1/2 tsp. (2 mL) dried dillweed
1 tbsp. (15 mL) capers OR 1 tsp. (5 mL) horseradish

- In a small bowl, mix together cream cheese and yogurt until smooth. Add remaining ingredients and mix well. Spoon into a small bowl. Garnish with a little grated lemon zest or chopped parsley.

- Serve with crackers, pita bread or crostini.

Makes 1 cup (250 mL)

Variations

Substitute canned **shrimp, crab or salmon** for smoked salmon.

Tuna Spread

To make this spread, look for the little sandwich-sized pop-top tins of tuna.

4 oz.	cream cheese softened	115 g
2 tbsp.	yogurt, mayonnaise OR sour cream	30 mL
3 oz.	can flaked light tuna with pepper, drained	85 g
1 tsp.	dried basil leaves	5 mL

- In a small bowl, combine cheese and yogurt with a fork until blended. Mix in tuna and basil. Cover and store in the fridge for 1-2 hours to blend flavors. Serve with crackers.

Makes 1 cup (250 mL)

Variations

SALMON SPREAD – Substitute canned **salmon** for tuna and use **dillweed** to replace basil. Try a splash of **hot pepper sauce or horseradish** with either spread.

Cook's Tip

Spreads can be a base for a tomato or cheese sandwich or a wrap, or spread on toast for a great go with for soup or salad.

SOUPS AND BREADS

CROSTINI

Serve these little toasts (crostini/bruschettas) with soup or salad, creamy cheeses or a bruschetta topping. Select a dense **crusty bread** *and cut ¹/₃″ (1 cm) slices. Brush 1 side with* **extra-virgin olive oil***, sprinkle with* **salt** *and toast until lightly browned. Use a toaster oven, toaster or broiler. Serve immediately. For* GARLIC TOAST*, rub bread surface with a cut* **garlic clove** *before toasting, or sprinkle very lightly with garlic powder.*

Tomato and Basil Bruschetta Topping

1 cup	diced fresh Roma tomatoes	250 mL
1	green onion, chopped, use most of the green part	1
1	garlic clove, minced	1
1 tbsp.	extra-virgin olive oil	15 mL
¹/₂ tsp.	dried parsley flakes	2 mL
¹/₂ tsp.	dried basil flakes	2 mL
	salt and pepper to taste	

- In a small bowl, combine all topping ingredients. For best flavor let stand 1-2 hours.

- Toast bread lightly, spread with bruschetta topping and serve.

- OR, spread topping to the edge of toasted bread, sprinkle with Parmesan and brown lightly under an oven broiler or in a toaster oven at broil setting.

Makes 1 cup (250 mL)

More Bruschetta Toppers

Sautéed **mushrooms**, especially sliced portobello

Garlicky **hummus** from your favorite deli, or homemade, page 45

Spread with a little **pesto** and grated **mozzarella cheese** – broil until cheese melts

Check the gourmet food section of your deli or supermarket and try a commercial **tapenade, caramelized onions or** chopped **black olives**

Mashed **sardines or** smoked **tuna** slices

Cook's Tips

Fresh **basil** is wonderful, dried basil is good too – make sure it is good quality and newly purchased. For the best flavor, make the tomato bruschetta topping a few hours or the day ahead so that flavors can blend.

Leftovers? Add to soups, salads, pastas or any tomato-based sauces.

WRAPS AS STARTERS

Easy to make and attractive on the plate, wraps are ideal starters – they can be made ahead and are easy to eat at stand-up-and-move-around gatherings.

Spread – Layer – Roll and Cut

PARTY PINWHEELS – Use large 8-10" (20-25 cm) **tortillas**; spread with something spreadable and savory like **herbed cream cheese, honey mustard or creamy mustard, cream cheese** mixed with a little **pesto or mayo** and **chopped chives or green onion**.

Layer tortilla thinly with 1 of the filling options below. Leave a 1" (2.5 cm) space on the far edge to seal the roll. Roll firmly, wrap in plastic wrap and store in the fridge until needed. To serve, cut in 1" (2.5 cm) slices. Discard the ragged end pieces.

Choose ingredients with complementary flavors and textures. Make 1 or make lots, make what you like.

Filling Options

Mustard and thinly sliced **ham** with a little chopped **lettuce**

Mayonnaise or spreadable **cream cheese** mixed with a few dried **cranberries**, topped with thinly sliced **turkey**

Herbed cream cheese and **smoked salmon**

Hummus with little bits of chopped **red** and **green pepper**

Mustard and **mayonnaise** and thin slices of **ham** and **cheese**

Cheddar cheese spread and tender baby **asparagus**, raw or steamed

Smoked Salmon Spread or Tuna Spread, page 48

Nutty Turkey Pinwheels

Here is a version that was a big hit at a party recently. Remember to leave a 1" (2.5 cm) space on the far edge to seal the roll.

- 4 oz. (125 g) **cream cheese**, softened, combined with 1 tbsp. (15 mL) of **mayo** and 1/4 cup (60 mL) of **cranberry sauce**.

- Spread on 2, 8" (20 cm) **tortillas**, sprinkle with chopped **toasted pecans** and layer with thinly sliced deli **turkey breast**, about 1/2 lb (250 g). Sprinkle with **salt** and **pepper**.

- Roll firmly, but gently. Wrap in plastic wrap and store in the fridge until needed. To serve, cut in 1" (2.5 cm) slices. Discard the ragged end pieces.

Variation

Layer **leaf lettuce**, chopped **romaine or iceberg lettuce** with the turkey. Roll as above.

Besides being comfort food, **soup can be a one-pot meal**, full of goodness from 3 or 4 food groups. To fit the criteria for quick cooking, these vegetable-loaded soups use purchased broths, canned beans and tomatoes, excellent products with loads of food value.

Raid your pantry and fridge to make quick, imaginative and tasty soup suppers. The amount to make is 8-12 cups (2-3 L), that's 4-6 servings at 2 cups (500 mL) per serving. Use your largest saucepan or, even better, your pasta pot. Sauté a few good things, add **broth**, **vegetables**, some fresh and some canned, **beans, grains** or **pasta** and **seasonings**. Simmer until the flavors are blended. Cool. Divide into 2-cup (500 mL) storage containers, label and freeze. **If stored in the fridge use the 3-day rule, "Eat it up within 3 days or throw it out."**

These soups qualify as "super-quick". They provide a meal for 2 or 3, or a meal for 1 plus a meal for another time. I can't guarantee that there will be no leftovers or extra ingredients, but these will be minimal, and when there is a portion left or part of a can, I have made suggestions for their use.

Homemade soup is comfort food, it evokes memories of coming home after a busy day, or a very blustery one, to the aroma of a soothing satisfying bowl of soup.

Investing a little time in making a batch of soup is an investment in future meals.

Instant Vegetable Beef Soup

In a medium saucepan, combine $1/2$ cup (125 mL) cooked crumbled **ground beef**, a 10 oz. (284 mL) can of **vegetable soup**, and $3/4$ can of **water**. Season to taste with **Italian seasoning**. Bring to a boil; reduce heat and cook for 3-5 minutes.

Makes about 2 cups (500 mL)

Cook's Tips

For **cream soups**, for convenience, use undiluted **evaporated milk**. It makes a creamy soup and doubles the food value of the added milk.

For **lower-fat** rich-tasting **cream soups**, use **evaporated skim milk**.

If your soup is too salty, add 1 potato, thinly sliced, to 1 quart (1 L) of soup. Cook until potato is tender, then discard potato.

SUPER-QUICK SOUPS

Combine canned soup with good things from the pantry and fridge.

Quick Clam and Corn Chowder

10 oz.	can EACH condensed potato and cream of celery soup	284 mL
12 oz.	can corn niblets	341 mL
5 oz.	can baby clams, undrained	142 g
1	soup can of milk	2

• In a medium saucepan, combine all ingredients and heat through.

Serves 2-3

Seafood Bisque

4¹/₂ oz.	can EACH crabmeat and small shrimp	128 g
10 oz.	can EACH cream of asparagus and cream of mushroom soup	284 mL
2	soup cans of milk	2
1 tbsp.	sherry	15 mL

• Drain and rinse shrimp. Pick over crabmeat and discard any shells.

• In a medium saucepan, combine all ingredients and heat through.

Serves 2-3

Quick Ham and Pea Soup

Hearty, satisfying and flavorful.

10 oz.	can condensed green pea soup OR yellow pea (split pea) soup	284 mL
1	soup can of water	1
1 slice	good deli ham, about ¹/₄" (6 mm) thick or 3-4 oz. (85-115 g), in ¹/₄" (6 mm) cubes	1 slice
¹/₂	small potato, cut into ¹/₄" (6 mm) pieces	¹/₂
¹/₄ cup	shredded carrot	60 mL
1	plum tomato, diced	1
splash	hot pepper sauce (optional)	splash

• In a medium saucepan over medium-high heat, combine soup, water and ham. Bring to a boil. Add potato, carrot, tomato and pepper sauce, if using. Bring to a boil.

• Reduce heat to simmer and cook, covered, for about 7 minutes, or until potatoes are tender.

Makes about 4 cups (1 L)

Lemon and Chicken Rice Soup

Tart, tasty and comforting after a long-day, hours of studying or a winter walk.

10 oz.	can chicken and rice soup OR chicken with white and wild rice	284 mL
1	soup can of water	1
1	lemon, juice of (or less if you prefer)	1
1-2	green onions, sliced (optional)	1-2

- In a medium saucepan, over medium-high heat, combine soup and water. Bring to a boil, add lemon juice and serve. Sprinkle with sliced green onions, if you wish.

Chunky Spicy Tomato Chickpea Soup in a Jiffy

Tangy and colorful, adding a grilled cheese sandwich makes this a satisfying meal.

14 oz.	can of chickpeas (garbanzo beans), drained, rinsed	398 mL
14 oz.	can of diced tomatoes, NOT drained	398 mL
10 oz.	can of tomato soup	284 mL
1-2	garlic cloves, crushed OR 1/2 tsp. (2 mL) garlic powder	1-2
1-2 tsp.	mixed Italian herbs	5-10 mL
1/2 tsp.	sugar (adds flavor to the tomatoes)	2 mL
	black pepper and hot pepper sauce to taste	

- Crush about 1/2 of the chickpeas on a plate with a fork. In a large saucepan, combine all ingredients. Bring to a boil, cover and reduce heat. Simmer for about 10 minutes.

Serves 3

Variations

Substitute canned **lentils** for chickpeas. Add a scoop of **hot salsa**.

Creamy Vegetable Soup

Milky vegetable soup, actually. This soup is made from items on hand. I use evaporated milk, see Cook's Tip on page 51, as it doubles the food value and gives a lovely creamy texture. To complete the meal have a pizza boat, page 102, or a quesadilla or 2, page 104.

10 oz.	can low-sodium chicken broth	284 mL
pinch	EACH of salt, black pepper and nutmeg	pinch
1	medium-sized potato, peeled, chopped into 1/2" (1.3 cm) pieces	1
1 cup	mixed frozen chopped vegetables	250 mL
2 cups	evaporated milk	500 mL
1 tbsp.	all-purpose flour	15 mL

- In a large saucepan, combine broth, salt, pepper and nutmeg. Bring to a boil, add potato and vegetables. (If vegetables are in large pieces, thaw partially under warm water and cut in half) Return soup to a boil; reduce heat; cover and cook 8-10 minutes, until potatoes are tender.
- In a small bowl, whisk together milk and flour. Increase heat to medium and add milk mixture. Cook and stir until heated through and bubbly, about 5 minutes

Serves 2-3

Creamy (or not) Pumpkin Soup

Very comforting, rich flavor and silky texture – make this quick version creamy or not – spice it up or serve it mild and mellow. Add more liquid if you prefer a thinner soup.

19 oz.	can of cooked pumpkin (15 oz./425 mL is OK too)	540 mL
3 cups	milk OR cream OR chicken stock OR 1¹/₂ cups (375 mL) EACH milk and chicken stock	750 mL
¹/₄ tsp.	EACH cinnamon and nutmeg, or more to taste salt, pepper and red pepper flakes to taste	1 mL

- In a large saucepan, combine all ingredients. Bring just to a boil. Cover and reduce heat. Simmer for about 10 minutes.

Serves 2-3

Variations

Add sautéed chopped **onion** and 1 crushed **garlic clove**. Top each serving with a spoonful of **sour cream or yogurt**.

CURRIED PUMPKIN SOUP – Add **curry powder or curry paste** to taste. Top with **garlic or herb croûtons** if you wish.

Red Bean Soup

A meal in a bowl, serve with toasted cheese bread or thick slices of whole-wheat bread.

14 oz.	can of diced tomatoes	398 mL
14 oz.	can of red kidney beans, chili style	398 mL
¹/₂ cup	finely chopped carrots	125 mL
¹/₂ cup	finely chopped celery	125 mL
¹/₂	small onion, finely chopped	¹/₂
1 cup	water, vegetable broth OR chicken broth	250 mL
¹/₂ cup	frozen kernel corn or canned niblets salt and freshly ground pepper to taste	125 mL

- In a Dutch oven or large saucepan, combine all ingredients. Heat over high heat until boiling. Reduce heat and simmer 10-15 minutes, or until vegetables are cooked.

Serves 2-3

Pictured on page 49

Variations

Add 4-5 cooked **tortellini** and/or a small amount of cooked ground meat to soup.

For leftover soup, cook some **rice**; heat the soup and serve it over the rice. Sprinkle a little grated **cheese** on top for a quick meal.

Cook's Tips

Use vegetables that you have on hand or the ones you prefer. Anything goes, **spinach**, **green beans**, **zucchini** or **potato** – **rice** too.

If you can't find chili-style beans, add ¹/₂-1 tsp. (2-5 mL) **chili powder** and ¹/₂ tsp. (2 mL) **basil** or **Italian herbs** when you add the salt and pepper.

Clam Chowder

Small amounts of vegetables added to canned basics make a delicious, satisfying soup.

2 tsp.	olive OR vegetable oil	10 mL
1/2	red OR green pepper, chopped	1/2
1	small onion, finely chopped	1
1/2 cup	TOTAL, very thinly sliced carrots and celery	125 mL
1	small potato, peeled and diced in 1/2" (1.3 cm)	1
10 oz.	can chicken broth	284 g
10 oz.	can baby clams	284 g
1 cup	whole milk, part cream is delicious	250 mL

- Heat oil in a large saucepan over medium heat. Add pepper onion, carrot and celery. Cook and stir until vegetables are soft and beginning to brown, about 5 minutes.

- Add potato and broth and bring to a boil. Cover; reduce heat and simmer until potatoes are soft, 7-10 minutes.

- Add clams, milk and cream, if using. Continue cooking until chowder is heated through. Do NOT boil once the milk is added. For a beautiful soup, garnish with chopped parsley.

Serves 2

Mulligatawny

This rich curried soup from southern India is very popular.

2 tsp.	vegetable oil	10 mL
1	boneless skinless chicken breast OR 2 boneless skinless thighs, cut into 1/2" (1.3 cm) pieces	1
1	small onion, finely chopped	1
1	celery stalk, finely chopped	1
1	medium carrot, finely chopped	1
1-2 tsp.	madras OR medium-strength curry powder	5-10 mL
2 tsp.	all-purpose flour	10 mL
2	big spoonfuls of peanut butter	2
3-4 cups	chicken broth	750 mL-1 L
1/2 cup	instant rice	125 mL
2 tsp.	lemon juice	10 mL
	sour cream and chopped peanuts for garnish	

- Heat oil in a large saucepan over medium heat. Add chicken; cook for 2-3 minutes. Add onion, celery and carrot. Cook until vegetables are soft, about 3 minutes.

- Push vegetables to the side and add curry powder. Heat until it becomes aromatic. Stir in flour. Stir in peanut butter. Remove pan from heat.

- Add chicken broth; return pan to heat; stir and heat to boiling. Reduce heat and cook for 3-5 minutes. Add rice and cook for 3 minutes. Add lemon juice. Stir and serve.

- Garnish with a dollop of sour cream and a few chopped peanuts.

Makes 4 cups (1 L) or about 2 servings

Pictured on page 49

Minestrone

Grated Parmesan adds lots of flavor to this thick Italian soup.

1 tsp.	vegetable oil	5 mL
¼ lb.	deli country ham, chopped in small cubes	125 g
1	medium onion, chopped	1
2 tsp.	bottled, minced garlic	10 mL
3 cups	chopped frozen vegetables OR a combo of what you have on hand – carrot, celery, cabbage, green or red peppers, broccoli and/or chopped spinach	750 mL
1 tbsp.	dried basil	15 mL
28 oz.	can diced tomatoes	796 mL
8 cups	broth OR 8 cups (2 L) water with 3 tsp. (15 mL) beef bouillon granules	2 L
1 cup	small pasta such as orzo OR elbow macaroni	250 mL
1 tsp.	salt	5 mL
½ tsp.	ground pepper	2 mL
	grated Parmesan cheese	

- Heat oil in a large soup pot over medium-high heat. Add ham and cook 2-3 minutes. Add onion and garlic; stir and cook for 2 minutes.

- Add vegetables, basil, tomatoes and broth. Increase heat; stir and cook until soup is boiling.

- Add pasta, salt and pepper and bring to a boil. Reduce heat and simmer for 10 minutes. If the soup is too thick add more broth or water. Freeze in family-sized batches.

- Sprinkle Parmesan over individual servings.

Makes 10-12 cups (2-3 L)

Variations

When you add 2 x 14 oz. (398 mL) cans of **white (cannellini) or red kidney beans**, rinsed and drained, this recipe makes a delicious soup/stew.

In place of ham, use ½ lb. (250 g) cooked, drained **ground beef, pork or turkey.** The addition of **chili-style red kidney beans** makes a southwest version – a new taste to enjoy.

VEGETARIAN MINESTRONE – Omit ham and add **white or red kidney beans**, OR use **lentils or chickpeas** if you prefer.

Cook's Tip

To have the Minestrone and Beef and Tortellini soups cooked and ready in 30 minutes takes some pretty fast chopping and stirring. The extra time invested means soup for dinner and extra meals in the freezer. These soups are my favorites for Friday suppers or Saturday lunches.

Beef and Tortellini Soup

On a cold night or a blustery day, serve this meal-in-a-pot.

2 tbsp.	butter OR margarine	30 mL
1/2 lb.	top sirloin, cut into 1/2" (1.3 cm) pieces	250 g
2 tbsp.	flour	30 mL
1	medium onion, chopped	1
2	celery stalks, chopped	2
1	large carrot, chopped	1
1 tsp.	bottled, minced garlic	5 mL
1/2 tsp.	dried powdered thyme	2 mL
1/2 tsp.	EACH salt and pepper	2 mL
2 x 10 oz.	cans beef broth	2 x 284 mL
3 cups	water	750 mL
28 oz.	can diced tomatoes and juice OR whole tomatoes, chopped	796 mL
9 oz.	pkg. beef tortellini	280 g
2 tbsp.	flour	30 mL
1 tbsp.	cornstarch	15 mL
1/2 cup	water	125 mL

- Heat butter in a large pot or Dutch oven over medium-high heat.

- Toss beef in flour and add to pan. Cook until beef is lightly browned. Transfer to a bowl.

- Add onion, celery, carrot and garlic to pan. You may need to add a little oil. Stir and cook until lightly browned, about 3 minutes. Stir in thyme, salt and pepper.

- Add broth, water, tomatoes, reserved beef and tortellini. Bring to a boil; reduce heat and simmer until tortellini are cooked, 10-15 minutes.

- To thicken, mix flour, cornstarch and water in a cup until smooth. Stir into the soup. Bring to a boil and boil for 1 minute.

Makes 10-12 cups (2.5-3 L)

Variations

Add chopped **green or red pepper** and 1 cup (250 mL) frozen **corn niblets** when you add the cooked beef and tortellini.

VEGETARIAN TORTELLINI SOUP – Use **cheese-filled pasta** and replace the sirloin with a can of **kidney beans**.

Cook's Tip

Refrigerate soup for up to 3 days; or freeze leftovers for another meal.

S A L A D S

Sometimes you want a little something more to round out a meal,or to serve alongside your deli choices or to go with that extra piece of chicken you cooked yesterday. Look here for salads to complement your meal.

Beginning on page 69, there are also some dynamite main-dish salads – hearty and delicious.

SUPER-QUICK SALADS

Look in your fridge and cupboard for the ingredients for a salad meal. Simply assemble the greens, fruits and vegetables. Add a little protein, like beans, meat, cheese, eggs or canned fish. For added crunch, top with toasted almond slivers, sunflower seeds, chopped peanuts, soy nuts or croûtons. Salads are a quick and delicious way to include several of the recommended 5-10 daily servings of fruits and vegetables.

Preparing Greens

Too often we avoid making salads because preparing the greens is too much trouble. Here is a **quick method**. Place a very large bowl in the sink, fill with cold water. Cut the base off romaine or leaf lettuce to separate the leaves; add the leaves to the water. Swish them around a little. Gently lift a few at a time and transfer to a spinner and spin dry, OR lift out a few leaves, shake a little to drain and place in a single layer on a clean kitchen towel, cover with a second towel and roll up loosely. Gently pat and turn the rolled lettuce to absorb most of the moisture.

Place dried lettuce leaves from either method in a plastic bag with a paper towel to absorb moisture. Store in the fridge. Lettuce will stay fresh and ready to use for 4-5 days.

Caesar in Seconds

For a satisfying, no-fuss Caesar, wash **romaine lettuce** and tear into bite-sized pieces.

Drizzle with bottled **Caesar dressing**, creamy or vinaigrette-style. Sprinkle with **garlic croûtons** and grated **Parmesan cheese**.

Variations

CHICKEN CAESAR – Top salad with grilled chicken

SHRIMP OR SALMON CAESAR – Top salad with grilled **shrimp or salmon**.

SALAD ADDITIONS

Add good things from the fridge or cupboard.

- Toasted **nuts or seeds** – chopped **pecans, almonds, peanuts, sunflower seeds**
- Fruit – sliced **pears, apples, oranges, grapefruit; strawberries, blueberries; raisins,** dried **blueberries,** dried **cranberries,** chopped dried **apricots**
- Thinly sliced **carrots, onions, rutabaga, cabbage, broccoli, cauliflower**
- Thinly sliced or small cubes of **hard cheeses;** crumbled **feta or blue cheeses**
- Small amounts of leftover **beans or grains**
- Chopped **hard-boiled egg,** small pieces of leftover **chicken, pork, beef,** deli **ham**
- Small amounts of leftover cooked **vegetables**
- For extra crunch, add **croûtons, Toasted Tortillas** cut into strips, see page 46, sliced **water chestnuts**

SALAD DRESSINGS

There is no need to load the fridge with bottles of salad dressings. You can easily make your own. Here are a few suggestions:

Instant Salad Dressings

Try these for economy, convenience and great flavor.

- Sprinkle salads with a little **olive oil**, a little **vinegar** (try **balsamic or cider** for a change) and a dash of **salt, pepper** and **sugar**. Toss gently and serve. Add more flavor with a sprinkle of dried **basil, oregano or Italian herbs.**
- For a Thai influence, try **oil, vinegar, soy sauce, lime juice** (**lemon or orange** work too), **sugar** and a sprinkle of dried **ginger**. Toss well.

Basic Vinaigrette

In a small bowl or cup, using a fork, combine 1 tbsp. (15 mL) **vinegar**, 1 tbsp. (15 mL) **water** and 2 tsp. (10 mL) **olive oil**. Drizzle over salad greens. Sprinkle with **salt, pepper** and **sugar**. Add a sprinkle of dried **Italian herbs, or** chopped fresh **basil** and **oregano**. Ever practical, I usually just sprinkle the ingredients over the salad and toss it a little – why dirty another bowl!

Variation

GREEK-STYLE LEMON VINAIGRETTE – Substitute fresh lemon juice for the vinegar. Use more or less to suit your own preference.

French Dressing

A good basic salad dressing, this can also be used as a basting sauce for chicken or steak.

1/2 cup	tomato juice	125 mL
2 tbsp.	olive oil	30 mL
2 tsp.	cider OR white vinegar OR lemon juice	10 mL
1/2 tsp.	Dijon mustard	2 mL
1/2 tsp.	sugar	2 mL
1/8 tsp.	garlic powder	0.5 mL
1/8 tsp.	dried thyme	0.5 mL
1/4 tsp.	salt	1 mL
	freshly ground pepper	

- Combine all ingredients in a jar, about 2-cup (500 mL) size, and shake well, or combine in a blender or food processor and process until smooth.

- Keeps for up to a week in the fridge.

Makes 3/4 cup (175 mL)

Low-Fat Cucumber Dressing

1/4 cup	low-fat mayonnaise	60 mL
1/4 cup	skim-milk yogurt OR buttermilk	60 mL
1 tsp.	lime juice (use grated zest, too, if you have time)	5 mL
1/4 cup	peeled, seeded, chopped cucumber	60 mL
	salt and pepper to taste	

- Combine all ingredients and serve with the Cobb Salad, page 70.

Makes 3/4 cup (175 mL)

Orange Ginger Dressing

Orange, ginger and garlic – use this dressing with mixed greens, mushrooms and mandarin oranges. Perfect, too, when you top salad greens with grilled chicken strips.

1/4 cup	orange juice, fresh or frozen	60 mL
1 tbsp.	vegetable oil	15 mL
1	small green onion, sliced	1
1 tsp.	minced ginger root	5 mL
1	small garlic clove, minced, OR 1/8 tsp. (0.5 mL) garlic powder	1
	salt and freshly ground pepper	

- Combine all ingredients in a small jar with a tight-fitting lid. Shake until blended.

Makes 3/4 cup (175 mL)

Pear and Onion Salad

Prepare a plate of **salad greens**. *Add half a thinly sliced* **Anjou Pear**, *several thin rings of* **red onion** *and a few toasted* **pecan halves**. *Crumbled blue cheese is good, too!*

Honey Dijon Dressing

1 tbsp.	water	15 mL
1 tbsp.	red wine vinegar	15 mL
2 tsp.	olive oil	10 mL
1 tsp.	honey OR brown sugar	5 mL
1 tsp.	Dijon mustard	5 mL

- Combine all dressing ingredients. Drizzle dressing over salad and add freshly ground black pepper.

Crispy Side Salad

The little packets of Ramen noodles are inexpensive and handy. They add a wonderful crunch.

1/2, 3 oz.	pkg. Ramen Noodles	1/2, 85 g
2 cups	shredded lettuce	500 mL
1/2 cup	peeled, cubed cucumber	125 mL
1	tomato, chopped in large chunks	1
1	green onion, sliced or a little chopped red onion	1
	chopped fresh parsley and mint (optional)	
	dressing of your choice	

- Break noodles into small pieces, about 1/2" (1.3 cm) in size.
- Combine all ingredients in a bowl. Drizzle with dressing; mix again and serve.

Choose one of the following salads to complement deli roast chicken or sliced cold meats.

Caprese Salad

An Italian classic from Capri – simple, colorful and delicious.

Alternate **tomato** slices with **mozzarella** slices. Drizzle with **olive oil** and sprinkle with chopped **basil or Italian seasoning**. Add **salt** and **pepper** to taste.

Variations

Drizzle with **balsamic or red wine vinegar**; sprinkle with a few **capers**.

Orange and Red Onion Salad

Slice 1 **orange**. Sprinkle with **Italian seasoning or** chopped **basil**. Sprinkle with 2 tbsp. (30 mL) chopped **red onion** – **salt** and **pepper** to taste. Drizzle with **olive oil** and **lemon juice or red wine vinegar**. This salad may also be served over mixed greens.

Variation for both salads

Add a few **Greek black olives**.

Moroccan Salad

Compose a salad of little mounds of some of the following on 1 or 2 **lettuce** *leaves. For a dressing, sprinkle with a mixture of* **lemon juice** *and* **olive oil**. **Salt** *and* **pepper** *and a sprinkle of* **cumin** *powder are good, too.*

> finely grated carrot
> grated red beets
> chopped radish, tomato and/OR red onion
> sliced cucumber
> fresh, blanched green beans OR asparagus
> sweetlet peas, thawed

Variations

MAIN-COURSE MOROCCAN SALAD – Add flaked canned **tuna**.

Broccoli Salad

So good! Enjoy a serving with chicken and rice. Add small cubes of Cheddar cheese to the remainder for a quick lunch. You may want to double this recipe to ensure leftovers.

2 cups	chopped broccoli florets and thinly sliced broccoli stems	500 mL
1/4 cup	raisins	60 mL
2 tbsp.	chopped red onion	30 mL
2 tbsp.	chopped red pepper	30 mL
1/4 cup	unsalted toasted sunflower seeds	60 mL
2 tbsp.	crisp crumbled bacon OR bacon bits (optional)	30 mL

Creamy Garlic Dressing

2 tbsp.	mayonnaise	30 mL
1 tbsp.	plain yogurt OR use 3 tbsp. (75 mL) mayonnaise total	15 mL
1 tsp.	sugar	5 mL
1	garlic clove, crushed (optional)	1
1 tsp.	cider OR rice vinegar (use lemon juice or pickle juice if you have no vinegar)	5 mL

- In a medium-sized bowl, combine all salad ingredients.
- In a small bowl, combine all dressing ingredients.
- Toss the salad with the dressing and enjoy.

Pictured on page 137

Variations

VEGETARIAN BROCCOLI SALAD – Omit the bacon. The flavor is still fantastic.

Use 1/2 **broccoli** and 1/2 **cauliflower or all cauliflower**.

Cook's Tip

This salad may be eaten when prepared or it may be stored in the refrigerator for a few hours to allow the flavors to mellow. Leftovers make a great lunch addition.

Greek Salad

This salad keeps well for 1-2 days in the fridge (without the lettuce), so you may want to make more than 1 serving.

	romaine lettuce	
1	green pepper cut into chunks	1
1/2	cucumber, peeled and cut into chunks (about 1 cup/250 mL)	1/2
2	thin slices of red onion, separated	2
1	tomato OR 2 Roma tomatoes cut into chunks	1
	Greek black olives, from your favorite deli	
1/2 cup	cubed feta cheese	125 mL
	dash of freshly ground pepper	
	a sprinkle of the oily juice from the olives and a little olive oil	
	a sprinkle of dried oregano OR basil (fresh is better)	
	Basic OR Greek-Style Lemon Vinaigrette, page 61	

- Prepare a bed or romaine lettuce and arrange vegetables on lettuce. Top with olives, feta cheese, olive juice, oil, herbs and dressing.

Pictured on page 119

Variations

GREEK COUNTRY SALAD – Omit lettuce and combine all of the other ingredients.

Vegetable Slaw

Slaws are good keepers. For 1 serving choose 1-1 1/2 cups (250-375 mL) total of finely sliced chopped **cabbage, broccoli, apples, cauliflower, peppers, carrots, radish, rutabaga** *and a little* **green onion.** *Any combo will do. Just use what you have on hand.*

Cider-Vinegar Dijon Dressing

2 tbsp.	mayonnaise	15 mL
1 tsp.	cider vinegar	5 mL
1/2 tsp.	brown sugar – white will do	2 mL
1/2 tsp.	Dijon mustard	2 mL
	sprinkle of salt and freshly ground pepper	
1 1/2 cups	chopped vegetables, see suggestions above	375 mL

- Combine dressing ingredients in a small bowl. Add vegetables. Combine and serve.

Cook's Tips

For 2 servings, or to serve with your hamburger tomorrow – double both the veggie and dressing ingredients.

When you have broccoli stems, peel and grate them on a medium-sized grater and make a broccoli slaw or add the grated broccoli to green salads.

For convenience, purchase a bag of broccoli or cabbage salad mix. For a tidier salad, and to make the slaw easier to handle with a fork, cut or chop the cabbage or broccoli in smaller pieces. I place the cabbage mix in a bowl and cut it with clean kitchen scissors. **No mess!**

Thai Salad

A little of this and a little of that can make a crunchy salad. For this salad you need 1-2 cups (250-375 mL) of crispy fresh vegetables, lightly toasted chopped cashews or almonds and a dressing with the flavors of lime and ginger – sweet, savory and sour flavors.

Try

sliced red and green peppers
peeled, seeded, sliced cucumbers
sliced green onion OR chopped red onion
halved or thinly sliced snow peas
sprouts, baby spinach leaves OR spring greens
chopped toasted cashews OR almonds
a little chopped fresh basil OR mint, if you have it, OR a
    light sprinkle of dried basil

Thai Lime Ginger Dressing

1 tbsp.	lime juice	15 mL
1 tbsp.	olive oil	15 mL
1 tsp.	sesame seed oil	5 mL
1 tsp.	soy sauce	5 mL
pinch	brown sugar	pinch
1 tsp.	grated fresh ginger	5 mL

- Combine vegetables and cashews.

- Combine all dressing ingredients in a cup and whisk with a fork. Pour a little over the salad. Toss lightly. Add more dressing if you wish. Sprinkle with basil.

Pictured opposite

Variations

Add sliced cooked **chicken** OR a few crushed **Ramen noodles**.

Rice Salad

Use leftover rice and veggies. Try it for lunch or with a piece of deli chicken for supper.

¹/₂-1 cup	cooked rice	125-250 mL
1 tbsp.	finely chopped red onion	15 mL
¹/₂ cup	or so, of chopped red, green and yellow peppers, combined	125 mL
	add any leftover vegetables that you may have OR	
	thawed frozen corn niblets OR sweetlet peas	
2-3 tbsp.	Basic Vinaigrette, page 61	30-45 mL

- Combine rice and veggies and add Vinaigrette.

Variations

Substitute **orzo, bulgur, barley or couscous** for the rice.

GREEK ORZO SALAD – Use 1 cup (250 mL) cooked **orzo**, a little finely chopped **onion, green and red pepper** and a few small **Greek olives**. Dress with 1 tbsp. (15 mL) **extra-virgin olive oil**, 1 tsp. (5 mL) **lemon juice**, a sprinkle of **salt** and freshly ground **pepper** and a pinch of dried **basil or oregano**.

MAIN COURSE – PASTA AND SALAD

Pasta Primavera, page 94

Thai Salad, page 66

Savory Focaccia, page 21

Lemony Rice Salad

Make this salad and enjoy it with deli chicken. The choice of vegetables is yours and depends on what you have on hand. It is best made in advance and chilled, but it is also very good served immediately. Leftovers may become a lunch dish or may be added to soups or salads.

¹/₂ cup	long-grain rice	125 mL
¹/₄ cup	EACH thinly sliced celery and carrots, cooked al dente	60 mL
1	green onion, sliced, use some of the top	1
¹/₂	tomato, cubed	¹/₂
4 tsp	extra-virgin olive oil	20 mL
1 tbsp.	freshly squeezed lemon juice	15 mL
	salt and pepper	
	chopped parsley, if you have it	

- Cook rice according to package directions. When cooked, spoon into a strainer and wash under running water. Drain. Transfer to a bowl.

- While rice is cooking, prepare and cook the vegetables. Cook until barely tender and still firm, al dente. Drain, rinse with cool water and drain again.

- Add vegetables to rice. Mix. Add oil, lemon juice and seasonings; mix again. Serve.

Variations

MAIN-DISH RICE SALAD – Add drained **tuna or salmon**, diced cooked **chicken**, cubed **cheese or olives**.

Use ¹/₂ cup (125 mL) **black beans**, drained, in place of carrots and celery. For color, add a little chopped **red pepper**.

Waldorf Salad with Chicken

This is a leftover chicken special or, if you have no leftover chicken, buy 4-7 oz. (100-200 g) of deli chicken.

1 cup	cooked chicken, chopped in small pieces	250 mL
¹/₂	green apple, cored and chopped in small pieces	¹/₂
1	celery stalk, sliced	1
2 tbsp.	chopped walnuts	30 mL
3 tbsp.	mayonnaise	45 mL
1 tbsp.	yogurt OR sour cream	15 mL
pinch	dried dill OR tarragon	pinch
	salt and pepper to taste	
	lettuce	

- Combine all ingredients, except lettuce. Serve on a bed of lettuce.

Variations

No lettuce? The salad is a nice accompaniment to a bowl of soup and a crusty roll.

Add halved **green or red grapes**. Try **blueberries** also.

Cobb Salad

A Cobb Salad is an organized chef's salad. The ingredients are presented in lines like the kernels on a cob of corn – pretty to look at, delicious to eat. I first had this main-dish salad in a restaurant in Santa Fe, New Mexico.

Pick up the ham or chicken at the deli or use chicken left over from another meal. Make it for yourself or expand it for a guest. The ingredients are your choice. My list is just to get you started. Allow 1/4 lb. (125 g) per person for the ham or chicken.

lettuce leaves OR coarsely chopped greens
cooked chicken OR turkey breast, diced
cooked ham, diced
canned tuna chunks
bacon, cooked until crisp and crumbled
hard-boiled eggs, diced
chickpeas OR kidney beans
chopped tomato
green onions, chopped, tops also
corn kernels
grated carrots
red OR green peppers, chopped
blue cheese OR cheese of choice, crumbled
ripe avocado, peeled, diced and dipped in lemon juice
cucumber, peeled, seeded and diced

- Line a platter with lettuce leaves or coarsely chopped greens.

- Choose small amounts of 5 or 6 of the remaining ingredients. Place the individual ingredients side by side on the greens so that they resemble the rows of kernels on a cob or corn.

- Use a creamy, commercial dressing or Low-Fat Cucumber Dressing, page 62, to drizzle over the salad.

Cook's Tip

When you want to make lovely straight lines of the Cobb Salad ingredients, place a piece of paper upright over the greens; add the topping ingredients in a straight row; move the paper along and add the next row of ingredients.

Salade Niçoise

Years ago when I made this salad, one of my children said, "You aren't going to eat that are you?" Yes, I did, and it was wonderful. I find that using oil-packed tuna, drained, adds more flavor than using water-packed for this recipe. You may use what you wish. Artfully arrange the ingredients so that they look inviting against the green romaine.

1	large serving of romaine lettuce, washed	1
1	potato peeled, cooked and diced	1
1/2 cup	barely cooked green beans, or more	125 mL
6 oz.	can of tuna, packed in oil, drained	170 g
1	hard-boiled egg, quartered	1
sprinkle	freshly ground pepper	sprinkle
drizzle	Basic Vinaigrette, page 61	drizzle

- Arrange romaine on a plate.

- Arrange potato and beans on lettuce. Add chunks of tuna and egg quarters. Top with pepper and Vinaigrette.

Variations

Add 1/2 tsp.-1 tsp. (2-5 mL) **curry powder** to Vinaigrette. Add 1-2 chopped **Roma tomatoes**.

Tuna, Chickpea and Fruit Salad

6 oz.	can of tuna, water-packed or oil-packed, drained, flaked	170 g
1/2 cup	chickpeas OR kidney beans	125 mL
1/2 cup	canned pineapple chunks OR chopped apple	125 mL
1 tsp.	lemon OR lime juice	5 mL
1-2 tbsp.	mayonnaise OR low-fat plain yogurt	15-30 mL

- Combine all ingredients. Serve immediately or refrigerate for 2-3 hours before serving.

Variations

Add drained, chopped **water chestnuts** for extra crunch.

Add some chopped **green onion** and/or shredded **carrot**. Add a tsp. (5 mL) of **Dijon** mustard to the dressing for added zing.

Cook's Tips

Use 3 oz. (85 g) cans of tuna, if you prefer, or you can use half of the larger size and save the rest for a sandwich or a melt.

Use any leftover beans in Chunky Spicy Tomato Chickpea Soup, page 55, Red Bean Soup, page 56, or Minestrone, page 58.

Curried Tuna Salad

This is delicious, crunchy and nutritious. A touch of curry in tuna salad means that people who think they don't like tuna salad love it.

Lemon Curry Dressing

1/4 cup	plain yogurt	60 mL
1/4 cup	mayonnaise	60 mL
1 tbsp.	lemon juice, fresh is best	15 mL
1 tsp.	curry powder	5 mL
7 1/2 oz.	can tuna packed in water, drained, broken into small pieces	225 g
1/2	unpeeled apple, chopped in small pieces	1/2
1/4 cup	raisins or chopped, dried apricots	60 mL
1	green onion, sliced, use some of the green top	1
	shredded lettuce	
2 tbsp.	chopped, toasted cashews (optional)	30 mL

- In a cup, combine dressing ingredients with a fork; set aside.

- In a medium-sized bowl, combine tuna, apple, raisins and onion. Add some dressing; toss and taste. Add more dressing if you like. Serve on a plate of shredded lettuce and top with toasted cashews.

Variations

CURRIED CHICKEN SALAD – Replace tuna with 1/2-1 cup (125-250 mL) **cooked chicken**.

If you have leftovers, make a sandwich with toasted **whole-wheat bread, tuna or chicken salad** and **lettuce**.

TUNA MELT – Toast 1 side of a thick slice of **bread**. Turn bread over and spread with **tuna salad mixture**; top with grated **cheese or a cheese slice**; broil in the oven or toaster oven until cheese melts and is bubbly.

Cook's Tip

Tuna can be purchased in single-serving pop-top cans and foil pouches. Look for the tuna pasta salads as well. These already-dressed salads have a pop-top and come with a little plastic fork – ready for a take-out lunch.

Beef or Turkey Taco Salad

This is a reduced-fat version of one of my favorites. Serve with lower-fat toasted tortillas or roasted tortilla chips.

	lettuce, chopped	
4 oz.	ground beef OR turkey	115 g
1	small onion, chopped	1
	sprinkle of salt, pepper and chili powder	
1/2-1 cup	chili-style kidney beans OR 7 oz. (200 g) can of chili	125-250 mL
	a little diced tomato	
	chopped green onion	
1/4 cup	grated Cheddar cheese	60 mL
	Toasted Tortillas, page 46, OR roasted tortilla chips	
	salsa and light sour cream	

- Prepare a plate of chopped lettuce.

- In a small or medium-sized non-stick pan, over medium-high heat, cook ground beef and onion until meat is no longer pink. Stir and break up as you cook. Place in a strainer and rinse with hot water. Drain well.

- Return meat and onion to pan and add salt, pepper, chili powder and beans. Cook and stir until heated through, about 2 minutes.

- Spoon meat mixture onto plate of chopped lettuce. Top with tomato, onion and cheese. Place Toasted Tortillas or chips around the edge of the salad.

GO WITHS – Little bowls of **salsa** and **sour cream**, chopped **avocado or guacamole**.

Pictured on page 85

Variations

CHICKEN TACO SALAD – Use leftover grilled **chicken breast** seasoned with **chili powder** or **cajun spice**. Add 1/2 cup (125 mL) EACH chopped **mango**, **red pepper** and **jicama**. Combine 1 tbsp. (15 mL) of **lime juice** with 1 tbsp. (15 mL) **vegetable oil**, 1/2-1 tsp. (2-5 mL) **chili powder** and 1/2 tsp. (2 mL) **sugar**. Toss with chicken mixture before spooning chicken over chopped lettuce. Add toppings as above.

VEGETABLES & RICE – MAIN & SIDE DISHES

Vegetables are a powerhouse source of vitamins, minerals, carbohydrates and fiber. They supply antioxidants and phytochemicals which help to protect the body's cells.

The Food Guide recommends 5-10 servings of fruits and veggies a day. A serving is 1 medium-sized fruit, or 1/2 cup (125 mL) chopped cooked vegetables or fruit, 1/2 cup (125 mL) chopped raw veggies or fruit or 1 cup (250 mL) of leafy green vegetables.

Choose fruit and veggies when you snack and try some of these recipes and tips to include vegetables and fruits in your meal planning.

EAT YOUR VEGGIES AND FRUITS

- Shop where vegetables are sold in bulk and buy what you like. Some stores sell portions of the larger vegetables, like cabbage and turnip. For small amounts and quick selection, look for the stir-fry packages of mixed vegetables or the salad-bar-type of display.

- Buy packages of **mini carrots** and include them in your lunches or as a "go-with" at meals.

- Try sliced **tomatoes** and **cucumbers or** strips of raw **turnip** and **celery** as starters or side dishes.

- Add grated **carrot** and finely chopped **onion** and **celery** to pasta sauces.

- For lunch, top a scoop of cottage cheese with thinly sliced **carrot**, **green onion** and **tomato** wedges.

- Cut up raw veggies and dip in a mixture of plain yogurt and a low-fat creamy salad dressing like Cucumber, page 62, or a mixture of low-fat sour cream and a sprinkle of salad seasoning, salt and pepper.

- Add sliced **tomatoes** and **cucumbers** to a tuna or ham sandwich.

- **From the freezer**, must-haves for me are **corn kernels**, sweetlet tiny **green peas** and **green beans**. I also like the **stir-fry** and **California-mix vegetables**, and the precooked **pasta and veggie mix**.

- Thaw a few **corn kernels or** tiny **green peas** and add to a salad.

EAT YOUR VEGGIES AND FRUITS *continued*

- Add vegetables to rice – try **green onion or peas**, 1-2 **tomato** slices.

- Fried rice is always made from precooked rice, add leftover or finely diced fresh vegetables to the combo.

- Keep fresh fruit on hand – crisp **apples** and juicy **oranges**, **bananas** too. Add fruit to cereals and add chopped vegetables to salads and pasta dishes.

- Serve an 8-oz. (227 g) can of **beans and tomato sauce** as a vegetable go with; use individual servings of **applesauce**, **pineapple or peaches** to accompany pork or ham.

Quick Fixes for Vegetables

- **QUICK CHEESE SAUCE** – Drain crisp-cooked **vegetables**, sprinkle with salt and pepper and add 2 spoonfuls of cheese spread or 2 slices of cheese. Cover the pot. Let stand for 1-2 minutes and serve.

- A squirt of **lemon juice** enhances most vegetables, especially asparagus and green beans. A sprinkle of **butter granules** will give you butter flavor without the fat.

- Thawed frozen vegetables can be added to **rice or pasta**, mixed with a little **salad dressing** and served as a side dish. Grated Cheddar cheese is good, too.

- Be inventive, add **tomato**, sliced **green onion**, shredded **cheese** and a sprinkle of **chili powder** to leftover rice and eat as a side dish

Quick Fixes for Couscous, Rice and Orzo

The mild flavors of couscous, rice and orzo invite savory additions.

- Use **chicken broth** in place of water
- Add a few **raisins**, **sunflower seeds** and a pinch of **cinnamon**
- Add a little sautéed **onion, garlic, green pepper** and **lime or lemon juice**
- Add sliced leftover **veggies** and a little **salt** and **pepper**
- For a hint of **curry**, cook **couscous** in heated **chicken broth**. Add 2 dried, chopped **apricot halves**, 1/4 tsp. (1 mL) **curry powder** and a pinch of **cumin**.

Cook's Tip

Canned tomatoes are the #1 staple in my cupboard. Their quality is excellent. Their multi-use in sauces, soups and stews assures good flavor, good value and convenience. They come crushed, diced, chunky, stewed and whole. Best of all, they are sold herbed, spiced, garlicky, roasted and with chili powder added. A 14 oz. (398 mL) can will provide 2 cups (500 mL) of instant sauce for pasta or use 1 cup (250 mL) for a pasta sauce and 1 cup (250 mL) to start a soup or add to sautéed chicken chunks.

SUPER-QUICK SINGLE-SERVING PASTA, POTATO, RICE AND COUSCOUS ESSENTIALS

Here are some single-serving basics. Sometimes we don't want to cook 2 or 3 servings. Rices, couscous and pastas are the building blocks for add-to's that make savory pilafs and quick pastas. Potatoes invite toppings or become essential main-course or side dishes.

RAMEN NOODLES – $1/2$, 3 oz. (85 g) package in 1 cup (250 mL) boiling water; cook for 2-3 minutes.

PASTA – 3-4 ozs. (85-115 g) spaghetti or fettuccini, or $3/4$ cup (175 mL) medium-sized shaped pasta such as rotini, fusilli or elbow macaroni; cook in boiling salted water for 8-10 minutes.

ORZO – Orzo is a rice-shaped pasta that cooks quickly and becomes a base for flavorful salads. Also add it to soups. Orzo, couscous and rice can be interchanged in most recipes.

COUSCOUS – This granular pasta is a nutritious staple food. Products vary. Be sure to read the method of cooking on the package. For most brands, simply bring 1 cup (250 mL) of **water** to a boil in a saucepan or microwave dish. Add $2/3$ cup (250 mL) **couscous**, a pinch of **salt** and a tsp. (5 mL) of **olive oil or butter**. Stir, cover and let stand 5 minutes. Fluff with a fork and serve. Makes 1-2 servings. Add **chopped vegetables**, **lemon juice** and crumbled **feta cheese** for a quick side dish or meal.

WHITE RICE – Bring $1/2$ cup (125 mL) **water** and $1/4$ cup (60 mL) **rice** to a boil; cover; reduce heat to simmer and cook for 18 minutes. For additional flavor, substitute **chicken broth** for water and add a generous pinch of **thyme or savory or Italian herbs** and 1 tbsp. (15 mL) **butter**.

INSTANT RICE – This is a good choice for singles. It is a good once-in-awhile staple. It's also a quick addition to soups and some casseroles. In a microwaveable casserole, bring $1/2$ cup **instant rice** (125 mL), $1/2$ cup (125 mL) **water**, a little **salt** and 1 tsp. (5 mL) **butter or margarine** to a boil, about 2 minutes. Remove from microwave and let stand for 5 minutes.

BROWN RICE – The newer brown rice products cook in about 20 minutes. I like the nutty flavor, especially in pilafs. For 2 servings, bring $1/2$ cup (125 mL) **rice**, $1 1/3$ cups (325 mL) of **water** and $1/2$ tsp. (2 mL) **salt** to a boil. Reduce heat to medium-low and cook for about 20 minutes.

BASMATI RICE – A very fragrant rice with a nutty flavor, from India, basmati rice is cooked like any other long-grain white rice, see above. This rice is sometimes called popcorn rice because of its aroma.

BAKED POTATO – Wash 1 large **baking potato** and prick with a fork. Cook on HIGH in the microwave for 5 minutes. Remove to a plate and cover with a towel as it continues to steam and cook.

CASSEROLE POTATOES – Wash 2 **potatoes** and slice $1/4$" (6 mm) thick. Place in a casserole with a sprinkle of **salt and pepper**, a sprinkle of **Mrs. Dash Original**, if you have it, and 2 tsp. (10 mL) **water**. Cover and microwave on HIGH for 5 minutes. A little **milk**, **cream or broth** may be used in place of water.

REHEATED COOKED VEGETABLES

- Heat a non-stick pan over medium heat; add a little **oil or butter**, add a little chopped **onion**. Cook 1-2 minutes; add **leftover cooked vegetables** and cook, stirring occasionally, until heated through.

- As the vegetables reheat, think about adding a little **basil or curry powder or** try a little grated **Cheddar or Parmesan cheese**.

- A small portion of vegetables can be heated in the microwave in 60 seconds.

OTHER WAYS TO USE LEFTOVER COOKED VEGETABLES

- Chop finely; add to salads, soups, omelettes, frittatas, stews; use to top pizzas.

- Room temperature or chilled asparagus and green beans are tasty side dishes.

- Chilled, canned, diced **tomatoes**, with a sprinkle of **basil or oregano**, **salt** and **pepper** make a refreshing vegetable accompaniment.

Baked Tomato Halves

- Cut 2 plum/Roma **tomatoes** in half lengthwise. Make a **Seasoned Crumb Topping** with 3 crushed **soda crackers or** a crumbled slice of **bread**, crust removed, mixed with $1/2$ tsp. (2 mL) **butter** and $1/2$ tsp. (2 mL) **salad herbs or Italian seasoning**. Spread on cut side of tomato halves.

- Bake in a toaster oven at 400°F (200°C) for 10-15 minutes, depending on the size of the tomato. If you are using the oven, bake tomatoes in a small dish at the same time as you bake your main course.

Variations

BAKED MUSHROOMS – Try the **Seasoned Crumb Topping** on large button mushroom caps or portobellos. Remove mushroom stems to make a pocket for the crumbs. Add the chopped stems to the seasoned crumbs.

Sautéed Cherry Tomatoes

Heat 1-2 tsp. (5-10 mL) of **olive oil or butter** in a non-stick pan over medium heat. Add 1 cup (250 mL) or more of cherry tomatoes, 1 chopped **garlic clove**, a little chopped **fresh parsley**, if you have it. Cook and stir until tomatoes are heated through but not bursting. Sprinkle with **salt** and **pepper** and serve.

Pictured on page 119

Greek Zucchini and Tomato

So good! If you have leftovers add them to a salad, sandwich or soup the next day.

1 tsp.	olive oil OR butter	
1/2	small onion, chopped	1/2
1	garlic clove, crushed	1
1	tomato, diced, or a few cherry tomatoes	1
1/2	small zucchini, about 1/2 cup (125 mL), diced	1/2
	salt and pepper to taste	

- Heat oil in a medium-sized non-stick skillet over medium heat. Add onion; cook and stir for 2-3 minutes. Stir in garlic.

- Add tomato and zucchini. Cook, stirring occasionally, until heated through, about 3 minutes. The tomatoes will be runny. If you use cherry tomatoes, cook until heated but not bursting. Season with salt and pepper. Serve hot or cold.

Variations

Substitute cooked **green beans** for zucchini and add **onions**. Sauté in a little **olive oil** and **butter**.

Stir-Fried Vegetables

A combination of vegetables, stir-fried, sauced or not, makes a quick-to-prepare medley of color, flavor and texture.

- Choose any vegetable mixture – **celery**, **peppers**, **green beans**, **pea pods**, **onions**, **cucumbers**, **zucchini**, **broccoli** and **cauliflower**, **cabbage** and **mushrooms**. Cut vegetables into even-sized strips or slices.

- Heat a small amount of oil in a non-stick skillet over medium-high heat. Add the firmest (longest-cooking) vegetables, like carrots, first; toss and cook. Add additional vegetables, keeping the pan hot as you cook and toss.

- When vegetables are heated through, cooked but still firm, sprinkle with a little **soy sauce**, **salt** and **pepper**, **sugar** and **ground ginger or 5-spice powder**. A squirt of **fresh lemon juice** is good too.

Lemon Green Beans

Cook fresh or frozen **green beans** in a little boiling water until tender-crisp, about 7 minutes. Drain, add a squeeze of **lemon juice** and a sprinkle of **garlic salt**. A little **butter** is good too. Garnish with toasted sliced **almonds**.

Carrots

Cook 1 cup (250 mL) of mini **carrots**, cut in half lengthwise, in a small amount of water until tender-crisp, about 5 minutes. Drain, sprinkle with a little **sugar** and just a hint of **nutmeg**. Adding 1 tsp. (5 mL) of **butter or margarine** makes them even better.

Sugared Sweet Potatoes

You will need 3 or 4, 1" (2.5 cm) thick **sweet potato** slices, 1 tbsp. (15 mL) of **butter** and 2 tbsp. (30 mL) **brown sugar**. Cook potatoes in boiling water until tender but still firm. Drain. Melt butter in a non-stick pan over medium heat. Add potatoes and sprinkle with sugar. Turn frequently, coating potatoes with butter and sugar until potatoes are completely coated and lightly browned, about 5-7 minutes.

GO WITHS – Meat loaf or sliced ham from the deli.

Veggie Chili 1, 2, 3

For this recipe choose already seasoned tomatoes or beans or both. **Chop** *and sauté the vegetables.* **Open** *the cans.* **Combine** *and heat. Ready.*

2 tsp.	olive OR vegetable oil	10 mL
1-2 cups	finely chopped vegetables – choose from onions, celery, green or red peppers, potatoes, carrots	250-500 mL
14 oz.	can stewed or diced tomatoes, chili-style	398 mL
14 oz.	can red kidney beans, drained	398 mL
	salt and pepper to taste	

Chili Toppings
chopped green onions, chopped tomatoes,
grated Cheddar OR mozzarella cheese,
sour cream, crumbled tortilla chips

- Heat oil in a medium-sized saucepan over medium-high heat.
- Add chopped vegetables; cook and stir about 5 minutes. Add tomatoes and beans. Bring to a boil. Reduce heat to low. Cover. Simmer for 5-10 minutes.
- Serve with your choice of toppings.

Serves 2

Variations

For added heat, add 1-2 tsp. (5-10 mL) **chili powder** and a pinch of **cumin** to the vegetable mixture, and/or a dash of **hot sauce**.

BEEF OR CHICKEN CHILI – Add about 4 oz. (115 g) of **ground beef or chicken** to the pan with the vegetables.

VEGGIE CHILI WITH A PLUS – Add soy-based ground beef substitute (**ground soy**).

Vegetarian Chili

Cumin adds an intense earthy flavor to this chili. Barley adds more goodness.

1 tsp.	cooking oil	5 mL
1/2 tsp.	red pepper flakes	2 mL
1/2 cup	chopped onion	125 mL
1/2 cup	chopped red OR green bell pepper	125 mL
1	small carrot, chopped	1
1	small potato (optional)	1
1-2 tsp.	chili powder, or more, to taste	5-10 mL
1/2 tsp.	ground cumin	2 mL
1	garlic clove, crushed	1
1/4 cup	quick-cooking barley (optional)	60 mL
14 oz.	can kidney beans OR black beans, drained	398 mL
14 oz.	can diced tomatoes	398 mL
1/2 cup	water OR vegetable broth, if using barley	125 mL

• Heat oil in a large saucepan or Dutch oven over medium-high heat. Add pepper flakes, onion, peppers, carrot and potato, if using. Cook until lightly browned, about 3 minutes. Push vegetables to the side to make a space in the middle of the pan.

• Add chili powder, cumin and garlic. Cook for 1 minute.

• Add barley, beans, tomatoes and water. Bring to a boil; cover and reduce heat to simmer. Cook for 20 minutes, until barley is tender.

• Serve garnished with a few crushed corn chips and a dollop of sour cream. Also see suggested toppings for Veggie Chili on page 79.

Serves 3

Another Serving

Leftover chili will keep, covered, in the fridge for up to 3 days, much longer in the freezer. For a second dish, bake a large russet **potato**, split and top with heated **chili** and a bit of **sour cream**. A Chili and Cheddar Quesadilla, page 104, is good, too.

Variations

Add a 14 oz. (398 mL) can of **chickpeas or lentils** to the chili or substitute chickpeas or lentils for the kidney beans.

Add a 12 oz. (341 mL) can of **corn niblets** to vary color and flavor.

TURKEY CHILI – Add 8 oz. (250 mL) of **ground turkey** when browning the vegetables.

BEEF CHILI – Add 8 oz. (250 g) of **lean ground beef**.

For more servings and a saucier chili, add a second can of **tomatoes**.

Cook's Tip

If you are short of time, omit the oil and the browning step. Just assemble all of the ingredients and cook.

Southwest Chickpeas with a Moroccan Twist

Served warm or cold, with rice or a salad or in pita pockets, this savory combo satisfies.

2 tsp.	vegetable oil	10 mL
1	small onion, finely chopped	1
1	celery stalk, finely chopped	1
1	garlic clove, thinly sliced (optional)	1
19 oz.	can chickpeas (garbanzo beans), rinsed and drained	540 mL
1 tbsp.	liquid honey OR 2 tbsp. (30 mL) brown sugar	15 mL
1/2 cup	raisins	125 mL
1/2 tsp.	cumin	2 mL
1/4 tsp.	EACH dried coriander, dried ginger and red pepper flakes	1 mL
1	lime, juice of	1
	salt and pepper to taste	
1	tomato, diced	1

- Heat a large saucepan or non-stick skillet over medium heat. Add oil, onion and celery.
- Cook and stir until the vegetables soften. Stir in garlic.
- Stir in remaining ingredients, except tomato.
- Reduce heat to simmer. Cook about 8-10 minutes, until beans are heated through.
- Stir in tomato. Serve warm.

Makes 3 cups (750 mL) – Store remainder for a second meal.

Pictured on page 85

GO WITHS – Rice or salad and bread.

Variations

For more color and vitamins, add diced **red, green and/or yellow peppers** to the celery and onions.

Adding a few dried **cranberries** will give this dish a fiber and Vitamin C boost.

PITA POCKET SPECIAL – Stuff halved **pita pockets** with **lettuce** and **Southwest Chickpeas**

Zesty Curried Chickpeas

Heat 2 tsp. (10 mL) **vegetable oil** with 1/2 chopped **onion** and 1 crushed **garlic clove**. Stir in 1-2 tsp. (5-10 mL) **curry powder or use vindaloo curry paste** for real impact. Add 14 oz. (398 mL) can of **chickpeas**, with 1/3 cup (75 mL) **chickpea liquid**, and heat for 8-10 minutes. Taste and add **salt** and **pepper**, a dash of **hot sauce** and, if using curry powder, 1-2 tsp. (5-10 mL) **ketchup**.

POTATOES

I prefer to have potatoes topped rather than stuffed. Here are 2 methods for baking potatoes, plus topping ideas to create a side dish or a meal.

Baked Potatoes

4	medium, oblong-shaped baking potatoes	4

Oven Method

- Scrub potatoes; prick with a fork or knife-point in several places. Bake at 400°F (200°C) for 45 minutes, or until potato begins to soften. Squeeze potatoes with your thumb and forefinger to check.
- OR bake scrubbed potatoes alongside a meatloaf or oven-baked chicken. At this lower temperature, 350-375°F (180-190°C), potato will take about 1 hour to cook.

Microwave Method

- For 1 large potato, scrub and prick well; cook on HIGH for 4-5 minutes. Wrap in a kitchen towel to continue the cooking process and keep warm.
- For 4 potatoes, arrange in a circle in the microwave, about 1" (2 cm) apart. Cook on HIGH for 10-13 minutes, turning halfway through cooking time. Wrap in a kitchen towel and let stand for 5 minutes to continue the cooking process.

Super-Quick Toppings for Baked Potatoes

- 8 oz. (250 mL) servings of **canned beans in tomato sauce or** 8 oz. (250 mL) **canned chili** – heat and top potato.
- 3 oz. (85 g) servings of **tuna**, **salmon or ham**, "sandwich mates". **Cheese** too.
- **Leftover tuna salad** topped with grated **cheese**; broil or bake until cheese melts.
- ¹/₂ cup (125 mL) **cottage cheese** mixed with a little chopped **broccoli, green onion**, **salt** and **pepper** OR **cottage cheese** and **cucumber**, **salt** and **pepper**.
- Leftover **chili** heated and topped with grated **cheese**.

Rösti

A crisp golden potato pancake from Switzerland.

Coarsely grate 1 second-day or cooled, peeled **baked potato**. Melt 1 tbsp. (15 mL) **butter** in a skillet, sauté 1-2 large spoonfuls of finely chopped **onion** and 1 tsp. (5 mL) of minced **garlic** for 2-3 minutes. Mix onion and garlic with potato. Add **salt** and **pepper** to taste. Melt more butter and scoop potato mixture into hot skillet. Flatten slightly to form a pancake. Cook for 2-3 minutes per side, until browned and crisp.

You may top Rösti with **smoked salmon**, **sour cream** and **capers** OR **curried vegetables** OR grilled or stir-fried **chicken**, or eat as is.

Variations

Add sautéed, crumbled **sausage or bacon or** sautéed **mushrooms** to potato mixture. Add flaked **crab**, **capers**, **lime juice**, chopped **green onion** and a sprinkle of **cayenne**.

Potatoes

Always bake 2 potatoes because that second potato is an investment in another meal.

- **To reheat** – Cut **potato** in ¹/₂" (1.3 cm) slices; fry over medium heat in a non-stick pan sprayed or coated with **vegetable oil**. Cook until lightly browned on both sides.

Toaster Oven Method

- Cut baked **potato** in half lengthwise. Score the top (make a series of shallow cuts in a crisscross pattern on top), spread with a little **mustard** and **olive oil**, sprinkle with **salt** and **pepper**. Heat toaster oven to 400°F (200°C). Cook potatoes until heated through, about 10 minutes.

- **HASH BROWNS** – Cut up second-day **potatoes** and cook in 2 tsp. (10 mL) **olive or vegetable oil** over medium heat until lightly browned. Add a little **onion** and diced deli **ham**, if you like.

GO WITHS – Make a frittata, pages 34 or 35, and add a green salad.

Oven-Roasted Potato Wedges

These are crisp, tender, low-fat potato wedges. Healthy French fries! It seems like a lot of trouble for 2 potatoes, but they are SO GOOD! And the recipe can be expanded for as many potatoes as you need.

2	baking potatoes	2
2 tsp.	vegetable oil	10 mL
	sprinkle of salt and pepper	
¹/₂ tsp.	your choice of no-salt-added seasoning blend	2 mL
	(I like Mrs. Dash's original)	

- Preheat oven to 425°F (220°C).

- Wash potatoes, cut in half lengthwise. Lay flat side down and cut each half into 4 wedges. Pat dry with a paper towel or a clean kitchen towel.

- In a small bowl, combine oil, salt and seasonings. Add potato wedges, stir and turn until potatoes are coated.

- Place potatoes, skin side down where possible, on a lightly oiled baking sheet or pizza pan. Bake until potatoes are browned and crisp, about 20 minutes.

Variations

A pinch each of **paprika** and **garlic powder** is a good seasoning or try **Italian herbs**.

PUNCHY POTATO WEDGES – Season with **chili powder or Cajun seasoning**.

OVEN-ROASTED SWEET POTATO WEDGES – Wash **sweet potatoes** and proceed as above. Try the seasoning variations.

RICE

Rice is nutritious, easy to store and easy to prepare. By itself, or combined with other ingredients, it is a side dish. The addition of meat, poultry, beans or eggs creates a main dish.

There are many kinds of rice and rice products. Read the labels to become familiar with them and with the cooking directions. For most recipes use long-grain white rice.

1 cup (250 mL) rice cooked in 2 cups (500 mL) water makes 3 cups (750 mL) cooked rice in about 18 minutes; 1/3 cup (75 mL) rice cooked in 2/3 cup (150 mL) water or broth makes about 1 cup (250 mL) cooked rice.

Brown rice and wild rice take longer to cook but they have more flavor and fiber than white and are often combined with white rice in pilafs and casseroles. Basmati rice has a lovely nutty flavor and cooks in 15 minutes.

Instant brown or white rice does not have the flavor or texture of real rice, but **enriched instant rice** does have an almost equal nutritional value. **Parboiled or converted rice** tastes like white rice, but it has almost as many nutrients as brown rice.

RICE DISHES

Here are 4 dishes that use cooked rice. You may have some leftover rice or you may have single servings stored in the freezer.

Rice and Bean Salad

1/2-1 cup	cooked rice	125-250 mL
1/2, 15 oz.	can red kidney beans, rinsed and drained (about 3/4 cup)	1/2, 540 mL
2-3	green onions OR chopped red onion, celery, red or green pepper and/or carrots very thinly sliced or grated	2-3
2 tbsp.	Basic Vinaigrette, see page 61	30 mL
pinch	garlic powder	pinch

- Combine rice and beans. Stir in chopped vegetables. Add vinaigrette and garlic.

Spanish Rice

Heat a medium-sized non-stick skillet over medium heat. Add 4 oz. (115 g) diced deli **ham or salami**, a little chopped **onion** and **green pepper**. Stir and cook about 5 minutes. Add a small can of **pizza sauce** and a pinch of dried **hot pepper flakes**. Heat until bubbly and serve over reheated **cooked rice**.

Variations

Add other veggies that you have on hand – a few frozen **corn kernels or peas** will do. Substitute **black beans** for kidney beans. **Good!**

VEGETARIAN MAIN DISH AND MAIN-DISH SALAD

Southwest Chickpeas with a Moroccan Twist, page 81

Beef Taco Salad, page 73

Fried Rice

Fried rice is always made with precooked rice. It is quick to cook and can be a side dish or a full meal.

1 tsp.	vegetable oil	5 mL
1	green onion, chopped	1
1-2 cups	cooked rice	250-500 mL
1-2	eggs, beaten (use a cup and fork)	1-2
	salt and pepper to taste	
	soy sauce to taste	

- In a medium non-stick pan, heat oil over medium-high heat. Add the onion, stir and fry for about 30 seconds.

- Add rice. Cook and stir until heated through.

- Add egg. Stir to mix through the rice. Cook just until egg is set. Add soy sauce to taste.

Variations

These are endless – look in the fridge. Add a few thawed frozen **peas or corn kernels**, leftover finely chopped cooked **chicken, ham, pork or shrimp**. Cooked crumbled **bacon** and chopped **peanuts** are good, too.

Quickie Pilaf

2 tsp.	vegetable OR olive oil	10 mL
1/4 cup	EACH chopped onion, celery and mushrooms	60 mL
1-2 cups	cooked rice, white, basmati OR brown	250-500 mL
2 tbsp.	water OR chicken broth	30 mL
1/4 tsp.	garlic powder	1 mL
1/4 cup	raisins	60 mL
pinch	cinnamon	pinch
	salt and pepper to taste	

- Heat oil in a non-stick pan over medium-high heat. Add onion, celery and mushrooms. Stir and cook until vegetables are soft, 3-5 minutes. Stir in rice until coated with oil, about 1 minute.

- Combine water, garlic powder, raisins and cinnamon. Stir into rice mixture. Season with salt and pepper and heat through.

Variations

Add 1/2 tsp. (2 mL) **cumin or curry powder** instead of cinnamon. Add toasted **pine nuts or slivered almonds**.

Add chopped, cooked **chicken, shrimp or leftover vegetables**.

Mexican Rice

No recipe needed – create your favorite version.

- Chop a little **onion, celery** and 1 **garlic clove**. Dump into a medium-sized non-stick saucepan with 1 tsp. (5 mL) **olive or vegetable oil**.

- Cook and stir over medium heat for about 3 minutes.

- Add ¹/₃ cup (75 mL) **rice**. Cook and stir for 3 minutes, until rice is coated with oil. Add ¹/₄ tsp. (1 mL) **salt** and a sprinkle of **pepper**.

- Add 10 oz. (284 mL) can of **tomato or V8 juice**.

- Bring to a boil, then reduce heat to a simmer. Cover and cook for 18-20 minutes, or until rice is tender. Add ¹/₂ cup (125 mL) cooked **kidney beans** if you have them.

- Top with grated **Cheddar cheese** and eat with **whole-wheat toast or a bun**.

Makes 2 cups (500 mL) – **to increase the amount**, add ¹/₄ cup (60 mL) more rice and ¹/₂ cup (125 mL) of broth or water.

Rice with Spices and Nuts

I like flavored rice dishes. This one is good with a grilled chicken breast, deli chicken or a fish fillet.

2 tsp.	vegetable oil	10 mL
1	small onion, chopped	1
1 tbsp.	slivered almonds OR chopped cashews	15 mL
¹/₂ cup	regular long-grain rice	125 mL
¹/₄ cup	raisins	60 mL
1 cup	water	250 mL
pinch	EACH cinnamon, cloves, turmeric and salt and pepper	pinch

- In a medium-sized non-stick saucepan, heat oil over medium-high heat. Add onion, cook and stir until softened. Add the remaining ingredients.

- Bring to a boil; reduce heat and simmer until water is absorbed and rice is cooked, about 18 minutes.

Makes 2 cups (500 mL) – This is a dish that I always make more of – **for 3 servings** cook 1 cup (250 mL) rice in 2 cups (500 mL) water. Increase almonds, raisins and spices just a little.

Pictured on page 119

Cook's Tip

To salvage burned rice, take the pot off the stove element; place a bread crust on top of the rice; cover and let sit for 5-6 minutes. The bread absorbs much of the burned flavor and smell. Don't expect miracles!

P A S T A

Most pastas are made from white flour. For added nutrition, choose fortified pasta; for more protein and fiber, choose pasta made with whole-wheat flour. Colored pastas are made with the addition of tomatoes and spinach.

Dried pasta keeps almost indefinitely and is less expensive than fresh pasta. It cooks in 7-14 minutes.

Fresh pasta should be used within a few days or frozen for up to a month. It cooks in 2-4 minutes.

We like pasta cold in a summer salad or dressed up for guests. The shapes and the sauces invite improvisation and add-to's.

Pasta will be your favorite super-quick meal. It can take less time to prepare the sauce than to cook the pasta.

Pasta is a good choice for both small and large appetites – just cook a bit more or a bit less!

Everybody loves pasta. It is inexpensive, low-fat, cooks quickly and adapts to a variety of sauces.

Pasta dishes are beautiful to look at and taste wonderful. Pasta comes in hundreds of shapes and sizes. There are excellent products available. Find one that suits you.

Entertaining at its easiest is a quick pasta dish, a big beautiful salad, a fresh loaf of crusty bread, and spumoni or your favorite ice cream with cookies for dessert.

Very Veggie – this chapter is loaded with vegetarian choices.

Fresh Tomato and Pesto Sauce

Make this pasta sauce from garden-fresh or hot-house tomatoes. It is delicious.

2-3	tomatoes	2-3
2 tbsp.	prepared basil pesto sauce	30 mL
1	garlic clove, minced	1
	salt and pepper to taste	

- Cut tomatoes in thick slices, cut slices into quarters to make chunks. In a small bowl, combine tomatoes, pesto, garlic and a little salt and pepper.

- Let the sauce stand at room temperature for 1-2 hours if you have time. If not – toss with hot cooked pasta and serve.

PASTA SAUCES – ALMOST INSTANTLY

Here are flavorful additions to your favorite pasta shapes. It is just like making your own "Side Kicks".

For 1 serving, cook ²/₃ cup (150 mL) of pasta shapes or about 3 oz. (85 g) of linguine or spaghetti. Follow the directions on the package. Drain pasta and save a little of the cooking water in case you need to moisten the pasta. Return pasta to the pot or dump into a heated bowl.

Add any of the following sauce combinations. For extra flavor use a good-quality virgin olive oil and a crushed garlic clove.

Pasta Sauces

HERBED OIL AND GARLIC – Add a little **butter or** a slosh of **olive oil**, 1 crushed **garlic clove**, 1 tsp. (5 mL) dried **basil** leaves or ¹/₂ tsp. (2 mL) **Italian seasoning**, freshly ground **pepper** and about ¹/₄ cup (60 mL) of freshly grated **Parmesan cheese** to the hot cooked pasta.

Add a little chopped **ham** and a few thawed sweetlet **peas** to the above sauce.

Sauté 1 cup (250 mL) sliced **mushrooms** and a little chopped **onion**. Add to pasta with oil and seasonings as above.

When you have **fresh herbs, add** about ¹/₂ cup (125 mL) chopped **basil or oregano** and serve with sliced tomatoes on the side.

Add a 3 oz. (85 g) can of **tuna**, a slosh of **olive oil**, **basil** and **cheese**.

Cook a little chopped **onion** in **oil or butter**, add ¹/₂ cup (125 mL) **tomato sauce**, ¹/₂ cup (125 mL) **cream or milk** and ¹/₂ tsp. (2 mL) dried **basil** leaves. Bring to a boil, simmer a couple of minutes and add to the cooked pasta.

Stir-fry a combination of **vegetables** in a large non-stick skillet. Add a little **tomato sauce or chicken broth** and a sprinkle of dried **basil** and **oregano**. Add drained pasta to the skillet; toss and serve from the pan.

PASTA WITH VEGGIES – Add **broccoli** florets **or asparagus** spears, cut in 1″ (2.5 cm) pieces, to the cooking pasta during the last 2 minutes of cooking time. Drain and add **oil** and **seasonings** as in Herbed Oil and Garlic above.

Simplest of all is 1 cup (250 mL) of your favorite **commercial pasta sauce**, heated, tossed with the pasta and topped with grated **Parmesan cheese**.

Cook's Tips

A sprinkle of sugar perks up tomato sauces. It balances the acid in the tomato.

There is no need to limit the choice of cheese. Use what you have on hand – **1 cup (250 mL) grated cheese is about 4 oz. (115 g)**.

SUPER-QUICK SPAGHETTI SAUCE SPECIALS

A jar of your favorite **spaghetti sauce** or a can of diced, seasoned or plain **tomatoes** on your cupboard shelf is a guarantee of a quick meal for 1, 2 or 3.

Here are 5 quick add-in ideas to perk up your meals. Try these sauces on filled pasta too.

For **1 serving** use 1 cup (250 mL) of sauce; for **2 or 3 servings**, use a 13½ oz. (375 mL) jar. When you have more than enough for 1 serving, remember that the sauce, enhanced or as is, can make a pizza topping or the base for a soup. Cover leftover sauce well and freeze or store in the fridge for a few days.

cook 1 serving of pasta as directed on the package

In a saucepan, over medium-high heat, heat the spaghetti sauce or diced tomatoes and add 1 of the following:

- Sliced **mushrooms, onions, peppers** and **garlic** sautéed in **olive oil** for a few minutes. Just until they smell good and look delicious, about 5 minutes.
- About 4 oz. (115 g) **ground beef or chicken** and a little chopped **onion** sautéed until cooked, about 5 minutes. Cook meat first and add sauce.
- 1 cup (250 mL) canned **white kidney beans** (cannellini) rinsed and drained and a pinch of **red pepper flakes**. Heat through.
- ½ tsp. (2 mL) dried **oregano or basil**, a pinch of **sugar**, freshly ground **black pepper**. Heat and combine with pasta; top with freshly grated **Parmesan cheese**.

For 2 cups (500 mL) of sauce, double amounts of herbs and sugar.

No-Recipe Presto Pasta

Cook 3 oz. (85 g), or about 1 cup (250 mL) of **small shaped pasta** in a large saucepan on the back of the stove. While the pasta is cooking, heat a medium-sized non-stick skillet over medium-high heat, add a little **olive or vegetable oil** and a few odds and ends of chopped **vegetables**. Toss and cook for 4-5 minutes. Drain cooked pasta and return it to the pot; add a little **olive oil or butter**, **salt**, **pepper**, dried or chopped fresh **basil**, grated **Parmesan cheese** and the cooked vegetables. Toss and serve with crusty bread. **Presto! Pasta in about 10 minutes.**

For the vegetables, try 1-2 cups (250-500 mL) of any combination of:
thinly sliced **carrots**, diced **zucchini**, sliced **cauliflower** and **broccoli, green onions, green, red or yellow pepper or frozen peas**.

Garlic and Oil Pasta

Over medium heat in a non-stick pan, sauté 1 crushed **garlic clove** in 2 tsp. (10 mL) **olive oil** until softened and lightly browned. Add to **pasta** with 1-2 tbsp. (15-30 mL) of **pasta water**, 2 tbsp. (30 mL) freshly grated **Parmesan cheese** and freshly ground **black pepper**.

Variations

CHEESY PASTA – Omit garlic and add more cheese, ½-1 cup (125-250 mL) grated **Cheddar or Asiago**. Toss pasta with **oil or melted butter and cheese**.

Cheesy Macaroni with Tomato and Green Onions

Use **elbow macaroni** and a few ingredients from the fridge and cupboard for this better-than-"KD" dish.

- Heat 1 cup (250 mL) EACH of **water and milk** in a medium-sized non-stick pan. Bring to a boil and add 1 cup (250 mL) **elbow macaroni**; return to a boil; stir and reduce heat to medium. Stir and cook until pasta is "el dente", cooked but not soft.

- Stir in 1 cup (250 mL) grated **Cheddar cheese**, and 1 tsp. (5 mL) **butter**.

- Add 1 diced **tomato** and a sliced **green onion**. Stir gently, cook for about 2 minutes, until heated through. Serve.

- **For a thicker creamier sauce**, cook pasta, milk and water a couple of minutes longer. Your milk choice can be **skim or whole canned evaporated milk**. Add 1/2 tsp. (2 mL) prepared **mustard** to perk up the flavor of the cheese.

Pasta and Spicy Tomato Sauce

Sauté 1/4 tsp. (1 mL) or more **red pepper flakes** in a little **olive oil**. Add chopped **onion** and minced **garlic** if you like. Add a 14 oz. (398 mL) can of **diced tomatoes** and a sprinkle of **Italian herbs**; heat and toss with hot, cooked pasta. Sprinkle with grated **Parmesan or Romano cheese**.

Try the already **seasoned tomatoes** – "stewed tomatoes or Italian spice" – or something similar. Good! Really Good! Super-quick Italian cooking! Leftovers are good cold or add them to your vegetable soup.

Pasta and Pesto

Toss hot, cooked **pasta** with bottled **pesto sauce**, about 2 tbsp. (30 mL) per serving. Sprinkle with freshly grated **Parmesan cheese**, **salt** and freshly ground **pepper**.

GO WITHS – Sliced deli meats or chicken and a salad of prewashed greens and sliced tomatoes.

Red and Green Pasta

In a non-stick pan over medium-high heat, sauté diced **red** and **green peppers** and a few sliced **mushrooms** in 2 tsp. (10 mL) of **olive oil or butter**. Cook until softened, add 14 oz. (398 mL) can **Italian stewed tomatoes** (canned tomatoes seasoned with herbs and spices). Stir and simmer to blend flavors, about 5 minutes. Add to pasta and serve. Top with grated **Parmesan cheese** and a sprinkling of **red pepper flakes**, if you choose.

Basic Tomato Sauce – No Garlic

I love garlic but not everyone does. Here is a basic no-garlic tomato sauce. Make a saucy pasta with 1 cup (250 mL) of sauce. Freeze remaining sauce for pizza or another meal.

1 tbsp.	olive oil OR vegetable oil	15 mL
1	small onion, peeled and chopped	1
1	celery stalk, finely chopped	1
14 oz.	can diced tomatoes	398 mL
1 tsp.	dried basil or ¼ cup (60 mL) chopped fresh	5 mL
¼ tsp.	sugar	1 mL
⅛ tsp.	dried hot pepper flakes (optional)	0.5 mL
	salt and pepper to taste	

- In a saucepan, heat oil over medium-high heat. Add onion and celery. Cook until soft, about 5 minutes.

- Add tomatoes, basil, sugar and pepper flakes, if using. Season with salt and pepper. Bring to a boil. Reduce heat and simmer for 5 minutes.

Makes 2½ cups (625 mL)

Variations

For a nutritional boost add a little grated **carrot** to the onion and celery and/or 1 cup (250 mL) of **cooked ground meat**.

Try sliced **mushrooms** instead of carrots. Yes, you can add **garlic** – add 1-2 cloves chopped garlic with onions.

Low-Fat Alfredo Sauce

This creamy sauce complements tortellini. Try it also with small shaped pasta and broccoli.

1 tbsp.	butter OR margarine	15 mL
1 cup	evaporated skim milk	250 mL
1 tbsp.	all-purpose flour	15 mL
pinch	EACH salt, pepper and nutmeg	pinch
1 tbsp.	freshly grated Parmesan cheese	15 mL
1 tbsp.	white wine OR lemon juice (optional)	15 mL

- Melt butter in a medium saucepan over medium-high heat.

- In a small bowl, whisk milk with flour, salt, pepper and nutmeg. Add to saucepan. Stir and cook until boiling. Remove from heat; stir in Parmesan cheese and wine, if using.

- Pour sauce over cooked tortellini or small shaped cooked pasta.

Cook's Tip

A slice of deli ham, diced, adds protein.

Pasta Primavera

This could become one of your standby recipes. It's mine. Put the pasta on to cook. Look to see what vegetables you have on hand. Chop enough to make about 1 cup (250 mL). Cook briefly, season and sauce. Add to the drained pasta and enjoy. I have included a method for frozen vegetables, using the California or Oriental-style mixes.

3 oz.	fettuccine or linguine (1 cup/250 mL)	85 g
2 tsp.	olive OR vegetable oil	10 mL
1/2 cup	broccoli OR cauliflower florets	125 mL
1/4 cup	EACH thinly sliced carrots, onion and celery	60 mL
	a few strips of red or green pepper, chopped	
1	garlic clove, minced	1
	sprinkle of salt and pepper	
1/4 cup	chicken broth, milk OR 1/2 and 1/2 cream	60 mL
2 tbsp.	freshly grated Romano OR Parmesan cheese, or as much as you like	30 mL

- Cook pasta in a large pot of boiling water, according to package directions.

- Meanwhile, in a large non-stick pan, heat oil over medium-high heat. Add broccoli, carrots, onion and celery. Cook and stir for about 3 minutes.

- Add red pepper and garlic. Cook and stir about 2 minutes. Lift pan from element and turn heat to medium if garlic appears to be burning.

- Add salt, pepper and broth. Stir and cook until heated through.

- Drain pasta well, place in a wide bowl or deep plate. Top with vegetables and grated cheese.

Pictured on page 67

Variations

Top with 2 tbsp. (30 mL) frozen **green peas**, thawed.

Add 1-1 1/2 cups (250-375 mL) frozen **California or Oriental-style vegetables** to the pasta water for the last 3 minutes of cooking. Return pasta and vegetables to a boil and cook for 3 minutes. Drain and add garlic, broth and cheese as above.

For more flavor, add a squeeze of **fresh lemon juice or** a slosh of **white wine** to vegetables, plus a few snippets of **fresh basil or** a sprinkle of **dried**.

PRIMAVERA WITH SHRIMP AND FETA – Add a handful of cooked **shrimp** and cubed **feta**. Just cook until heated through.

Cook's Tip

Italian Sausage – It is difficult to buy only 1 or 2 Italian sausages. Here are a couple of meal ideas to solve the problem.

Cut the sausage in 1/2" (1.3 cm) slices. Cook in a non-stick pan lightly sprayed with oil. Use half the cooked sausage for Italian Sausage with Pasta, page 96, and freeze half in a small self-sealing freezer bag. Use to top a pizza or add to macaroni and cheese or Minestrone Soup, page 58.

Macaroni and Cheese

I have never been a fan of K.D. but I love macaroni and cheese. This version is almost as quick as the K.D. special and it is certainly superior in flavor and texture.

1 cup	elbow macaroni OR small fusilli (3 oz./85 grams)	250 mL
1 tbsp.	butter OR margarine	15 mL
1 tbsp.	flour	15 mL
1 cup	milk – skim if you choose, 2% is nicer	250 mL
1 cup	grated medium or sharp Cheddar cheese	250 mL
	salt and pepper to taste	

- In a large pot of boiling salted water, cook macaroni until tender but still firm, about 7 minutes.
- While macaroni is cooking, melt butter in a small saucepan over medium-high heat; add flour and blend with a fork or flat whisk. Gradually stir in milk. Bring to a boil.
- Add cheese; reduce heat and stir until cheese is melted. Drain macaroni and stir into cheese sauce.

GO WITHS – A crisp salad or sliced tomatoes and cucumbers.

Variations

Add a few **broccoli** florets to the macaroni and water during the last 2 minutes of cooking time.

Add a sliced **Roma tomato** and/or a little chopped **ham or** cooked **sausage**.

DRESSED-UP MACARONI AND CHEESE – Pour macaroni and cheese into an ovenproof casserole, top with buttered crumbs and brown under an oven broiler or the broil setting of a toaster oven – watch, it only takes 1-2 minutes.

BUTTERED CRUMBS – Crush 4 **soda crackers** in a sandwich bag, use a rolling pin or wine bottle. Mix crumbs with 2 tsp. (10 mL) **soft butte**r, using your fingers is easiest. Sprinkle crumbs on macaroni and cheese; brown lightly under a broiler.

Pasta with Tuna and Garlic

When you want the rich flavor of tuna, choose a good-quality brand, packed in oil. This garlicky dish is quick, inexpensive and made from items in the cupboard.

3-4 oz.	linguine or fusilli	85-115 g
6 oz.	can solid tuna packed in oil	170 g
1	garlic clove, minced	1
1/2 tsp.	dried dill OR basil	2 mL
	salt and freshly ground pepper to taste	

- Cook pasta as directed on the package.
- Meanwhile, in a medium-sized bowl, combine tuna, garlic and dill. Use a fork to break up tuna. Add hot drained pasta and 1-2 tbsp. (15-30 mL) of pasta water. Toss and serve.

GO WITHS – A crisp green salad and Savory Focaccia, page 21.

Chicken Pasta Sauce

This thick chunky family favorite uses prepared spaghetti sauce.

2 tsp.	vegetable oil	10 mL
1/2 lb.	ground chicken OR chicken breast, cut in small pieces	250 g
14 oz.	can spaghetti sauce or 2 cups (500 mL) from a jar	398 mL
1 tsp.	EACH basil, oregano and sugar	5 mL
pinch	hot pepper flakes	pinch
	salt and pepper to taste	

- Heat oil in a large non-stick pan on medium-high. Add chicken; cook and stir. Use a wooden spatula to break up the chicken as it cooks. Drain and blot with a paper towel to remove excess fat.

- Add spaghetti sauce, herbs, sugar and pepper flakes.

- Heat to boiling. Reduce heat; cover and simmer for 10 minutes, stirring often. Serve with your favorite pasta.

Serves 2 – **for 4 servings**, use 1 lb. (500 g) ground chicken or beef; **for 6 servings**, add a second can of spaghetti sauce.

Variations

Use lean ground beef for BEEF PASTA SAUCE. Both sauces invite the addition of vegetables – choose **green and red peppers**, **onions**, grated **carrots** and chunks of **zucchini**.

Italian Sausage with Pasta

There are 2 ways to make this pasta dish. Use pizza sauce or 1/2 a can of seasoned tomatoes. Pizza sauce means no leftovers. The diced tomatoes have a fresher flavor and leave you with a half can to use in a soup or stew. I prefer the canned tomatoes.

1 cup	fusilli, cooked according to package directions	250 mL
1 tsp.	olive oil	5 mL
1	Italian sausage, about 4 oz. (115 g), cut into bite-sized pieces	1
1 cup	combined, chopped green pepper, red pepper and onion	250 mL
1/2, 14 oz.	can Italian diced tomatoes OR 7 1/2 oz. (213 mL) can	1/2, 398 g
	of pizza sauce and a little pasta water	
	a slosh of red wine	
pinch	dried basil	pinch

- Heat a medium-sized saucepan or non-stick skillet over medium heat. Add oil, sausage, peppers and onions. Cook and stir until sausage is cooked, about 10 minutes.

- Add tomatoes or sauce, wine and basil. Cook and stir until heated through. Toss with drained fusilli and serve.

Cook's Tip

I like the convenience of small cans of pizza or tomato sauce. Having 1-2 cans in the cupboard means almost instant pizza or pasta. A little basil and lemon juice perks up the flavor.

Tuscany Chicken and Tomatoes

The dump-it-all-in-one-pot style, plus no browning of the chicken, makes this recipe super-quick.

1 lb.	or 6 pieces boneless, skinless chicken thighs	500 g
1 tsp.	Italian herb seasoning	5 mL
2 cups	frozen mixed vegetables (from a 1 lb. [500 g] package of international mix, including broccoli, cauliflower and carrots)	500 mL
2 x 14 oz.	can diced or Italian-style tomatoes	2 x 398 mL
	salt and pepper to taste	
	cooked pasta to serve 4 or 6, about 1 lb./500 g, (try penne, fusilli or linguini)	

- Trim fat from chicken thighs and cut into bite-sized pieces.

- Put chicken and remaining ingredients into a pot and bring to a boil. Stir; cover; reduce heat to a simmer. Cook for 5-10 minutes, until chicken is fork-tender.

- Season with salt and pepper. Serve with the pasta.

Serves 4-6 – **to serve 2-3**, halve the recipe.

GO WITHS – Chunks of fresh whole-grain bread or garlic bread and a Greek Salad, page 65.

Variations

For a more intense flavor, add 1/4-1/2 tsp. (1-2 mL) of **dried hot pepper flakes** and 2 cloves of chopped **garlic** when you combine the ingredients in the pot to cook.

If you have fresh vegetables on hand, you can use a variety of chopped vegetables, e.g., **broccoli**, **cauliflower**, **carrots**, **red bell peppers**, etc., **or use only broccoli** if you prefer.

Cook's Tip

Leftover cooked pasta can be stored, covered, in the fridge for a couple of days or in the freezer for weeks. To reheat, microwave for 3-4 minutes or dip into boiling water until heated through, about 3 minutes.

FILLED PASTAS

Look for the little pockets of ravioli and tortellini. They are usually displayed in a cooler near the dairy products. Choose meat, cheese or spinach-filled pastas – 1-1½ cups (250-375 mL) makes a generous single serving.

Cook in boiling salted water according to package directions, for about 8 minutes.

For a quick dress-up use any of the quick sauces on pages 89-91.

Ravioli – Super-Quick

Count out the number of ravioli for 1 serving. Save the rest for another meal or add them to a soup. I cook an overflowing cupful (300 mL).

1 serving of cheese or meat ravioli

Basil Tomato Sauce

14 oz.	can diced tomatoes – Italian style – use part of the can if you want a smaller portion	398 mL
½ tsp.	dried basil OR oregano flakes	2 mL
¼ cup	grated mozzarella OR Cheddar cheese	60 mL

- Cook ravioli according to package directions.

- Meanwhile, heat tomatoes and basil in a small pot or in a bowl in the microwave. Drain cooked pasta and add tomatoes, basil and cheese.

GO WITHS – A salad and garlic toast.

Creamy Mushroom Sauce for Filled Pasta

Here is a quick creamy sauce to serve with small amounts of pasta or with cooked filled pasta.

1 tbsp.	butter	15 mL
2	sliced green onions OR 2 tbsp. (30 mL) chopped onion	2
½ cup	sliced mushrooms	125 mL
½ cup	cream OR evaporated milk	125 mL
1 tbsp.	dried tarragon	15 mL
½ tsp.	fresh lemon juice	2 mL

- Melt butter in a small saucepan over medium-high heat. Add onions and mushrooms. Sauté until soft and beginning to brown.

- Add cream and tarragon (crush the tarragon with your fingers as you add it).

- Heat to boiling, then reduce heat to low and simmer 3-4 minutes.

- Stir in lemon juice and pour sauce over cooked ravioli or tortellini.

Creamy Tortellini with Mushrooms and Tomatoes

Prepare the creamy sauce while the tortellini cooks – your meal is ready in minutes.

1 serving tortellini OR ravioli – an overflowing cupful

Mushroom Tomato Sauce

2 tsp.	olive oil OR butter	10 mL
1 cup	sliced mushrooms	250 mL
1/2 cup	milk OR cream	125 mL
1/2 cup	chicken OR vegetable broth OR more milk	125 mL
2 tbsp.	freshly grated Parmesan cheese	30 mL
pinch	EACH dried basil and lemon zest	pinch
	a squeeze of fresh lemon juice	
1	plum tomato, diced	1

- Cook tortellini according to package directions.

- Meanwhile, in a medium-sized non-stick pan, heat oil over medium-high heat. Add mushrooms; cook until soft and beginning to brown at the edges.

- Add milk, broth and cheese. Cook and stir until cheese is melted. Add basil, zest and lemon juice.

- Combine with drained tortellini. Top with chopped tomato.

Variations

Add 1 cup (250 mL) chopped **broccoli** florets to the pasta water the last minute of cooking. Add a minced **garlic** clove to the pan with the mushrooms.

Tortellini with Tomatoes and Zucchini

4 1/2 oz.	cheese tortellini OR ravioli, 1/2 of a 9 oz. (280 g) pkg.	140 g
2 tsp	olive OR vegetable oil	15 mL
1	garlic clove, minced OR 1/2 tsp. (2 mL) bottled, minced	1
2	small zucchini, quartered lengthwise and cut into 1/2" (1.3 cm) slices	2
1	large tomato, peeled and diced	1
1/2 cup	chicken broth, vegetable broth OR water	125 mL
1 tsp	dried basil or 2 tbsp. (30 mL) chopped fresh salt and pepper to taste	5 mL

- Cook tortellini according to package directions.

- Meanwhile, heat oil in a large, non-stick pan over medium-high heat. Add garlic and zucchini; cook and stir for 5 minutes.

- Add tomato, broth and basil. Cook and stir for 5 minutes; add salt and pepper. Pour sauce over tortellini and serve.

P I Z Z A &
T O R T I L L A S

*P*izza is the #1 take-home from the supermarket and the #1 selection for food delivery. Why? Because it is good, nutritious, easy to eat, almost no clean up, except for the big box that won't fit in the garbage can or even go down the chute in apartment buildings.

Make a better pizza – make your own!

A pizza base can be anything you choose. Our family always made pizza boats – a French loaf cut in half lengthwise, layered with good things and baked. You might choose precooked pizza crusts, Pillsbury pizza dough, a pita, a flat Italian bread or a tortilla. Make pizza for supper; make extra and take a piece for lunch or have it with soup or salad the next day.

Very Veggie – this chapter is loaded with vegetarian choices.

SUPER-QUICK PIZZAS

Brush a pizza base with a little **tomato or pasta sauce, pesto, mayonnaise or cheese spread**. Add your favorite topping or toppings and a little **grated cheese**. Cook pizza at 425°F (220°C) for 8-12 minutes, until the toppings are heated through and cheese is melted and bubbly. Tortilla pizzas will take a little less time.

For the best pizzas, KEEP IT SIMPLE, 2 or 3 toppings will do. Bake on the bottom rack of the oven for a crisp crust.

Try some of these combos

MARGHERITA PIZZA – Spread **pizza base** with **tomato sauce or pizza sauce**. Add **sliced Roma tomatoes**; a sprinkle of dried **basil or Italian herbs**, grated **mozzarella** cheese and freshly grated **Parmesan**. Bake as above.

MUSHROOM AND PEPPERONI – Spread **pizza base** with **tomato sauce**; add a few thin slices of **pepperoni**, thinly sliced **mushrooms** and grated **mozzarella** cheese. Bake as above.

CANADIAN BACON AND PINEAPPLE – Spread **pizza base** with **tomato sauce**; add a few slices coarsely chopped **Canadian bacon** (or precooked side bacon), a few **pineapple tidbits** and grated **mozzarella** cheese. Bake as above.

Cook's Tips

To fully enjoy the flavors of the pizza don't overload the crust, the distinct flavors and textures of the crust, oil, garlic, vegetables and cheese should shine through.

Pizza Primavera

*I like to keep a ready-to-bake **tube of pizza dough** in the fridge. I can almost always find on-hand toppings in the fridge and on cupboard shelves. A bonus is that visiting friends enjoy the results and like to help. One tube of pizza dough makes about 4 servings.*

1	medium onion thinly sliced	1
4 ozs.	mushrooms, sliced (about 1 cup [250 mL])	115 g
1/2	red bell pepper, sliced	1/2
1/2	green bell pepper, sliced, OR 1 cup (250 mL) broccoli florets	1/2
1 tube	pizza dough	1 tube
7 1/2 oz.	can of pizza sauce OR tomato sauce (part of the can only)	213 mL
1-2 cups	pizza cheese OR a mixture of grated Cheddar and mozzarella	250-500 mL

- To make Pizza Primavera follow package directions and use ingredients above. Sautéing vegetables in a lightly oiled pan for 2-3 minutes before adding to pizza adds flavor and ensures more evenly cooked vegetables on top of the pizza.

Variations

Follow package directions using one of the topping combos on the previous page.

WHITE PIZZA

White pizza (Pizza Bianca) is pizza without tomato sauce. If you don't like tomatoes or tomato sauce, this is the pizza for you. I find it makes a nice change from the usual. I sometime make a broccoli or shrimp pizza to have with salad or soup.

MUSHROOM AND HAM PIZZA – Cover **pizza base** with a little **mustard or mayo** and thinly sliced **mushrooms**. Add strips of deli **ham,** 4 oz. (115 g), and a covering of grated **mozzarella or Swiss cheese**. Bake as on page 90.

BROCCOLI PIZZA – Brush **pizza base** with extra-virgin **olive oil or margarine**; add 2-3 chopped **broccoli** florets, a sprinkle of **salt** and freshly ground **pepper**; top with grated **Swiss or mozzarella cheese**. Bake as on page 90.

DOUBLE CHEESE PIZZA – Lightly spread **pizza base** with **pesto**; dot with small chunks of **Roma Tomato** and sprinkle with **mozzarella** and freshly grated **Parmesan cheese**. Bake as on page 90.

SHRIMP PIZZA – Sauté a few strips of **red pepper** in **olive oil**, add 1 can drained **shrimp**; sprinkle with a little **lemon juice**, **salt** and **pepper**. Spread over the **pizza base**; top with grated **mozzarella** cheese. Bake as on page 90.

PORTOBELLO MUSHROOMS – This is the best pizza. Gently sauté **mushroom slices, red onion rings** and a minced **garlic clove** in **olive oil** for about 5 minutes. Spread over **pizza base**; add small chunks of **goat cheese or mozzarella**. Bake as on page 90.

Cook's Tip

Split English muffins, tortillas, hamburger bun halves and pitas may be used to make individual snack pizzas.

Pizza Boats

This is a family favorite – we use French bread cut in half horizontally. Serve it with a bowl of soup and it's a meal. Cut in 3" (8 cm) pieces, it's a great snack or appetizer. For a single serving, use a baguette or any suitably sized crusty roll cut in half and topped.

1 tsp.	vegetable oil OR olive oil	5 mL
1-2 cups	combined, chopped onion, mushrooms, red pepper	250-500 mL
1/2 tsp.	dried Italian herbs	2 mL
	sprinkle of salt and pepper	
1/2	baguette OR 2 crusty rolls	1/2
1/4 cup	pizza sauce OR leftover pasta sauce	60 mL
	cheese spread	
1 cup	shredded mozzarella OR pizza cheese	250 mL

- In large non-stick skillet, heat vegetable oil over medium heat; cook chopped onion, sliced mushrooms, red pepper, dried Italian herbs, salt and pepper, stirring occasionally, until no liquid remains, about 6 minutes, add pizza sauce.

- Cut baguette or buns horizontally in half. Spread with cheese spread; add vegetables and sprinkle with shredded cheese.

- Place on a baking sheet. Bake at 400°F (200°C) until cheese is melted and baguette is crisp, about 15 minutes.

Variations

Try these toppings on premade pizza crusts or the "dough boy" pizza crusts sold in the dairy case at the supermarket. Pack the leftovers for lunch or serve with a bowl of soup for another meal.

- A little **olive oil**, thinly sliced **tomatoes** (or canned Italian plum tomatoes, drained and chopped) a sprinkle of **pepper**, shredded **mozzarella cheese** and grated **Parmesan**.

- A little **olive oil**, thinly sliced **salami or pepperoni**, chopped **onion** OR **tomato sauce** and grated **cheese**, **oregano or basil,** if you like.

- Sautéed **red pepper**, **red onion** and **broccoli**, a little **pizza sauce** and grated **cheese**.

- Anything goes, try **ham** and **pineapple** OR leftover **veggies**, **pizza sauce** and cheese OR **pasta meat sauce** with **cheese and garlic** – as you like it.

- CHILI BOAT – Spread **buns or bread** with leftover **chili**, top with grated **cheese** and bake or broil.

TORTILLAS

To add variety to your super-quick meals and snacks, make sure you have a package of flour tortillas in the fridge or freezer. A few favorite ingredients and a little creativity and your wrap, burrito, fajita, pizza or quesadilla is ready.

Tortillas come in many varieties: originals, whole-wheat, tomato, spinach, herb, etc.

2 large filled tortillas make 1 generous serving. A package of 10 is a lot for 1 person. The good thing is that they keep for weeks in the fridge or months in the freezer. Be sure to seal the bag.

Tortilla Pizza

This snack/lunch is quick as a wink to make. Tortillas with cheese only are also good.

2	whole-wheat OR plain flour tortillas	2
1/2, 14 oz	can, fat-free refried beans	1/2, 398 mL
1/4 cup	medium salsa	60 mL
1	Roma tomato, thinly sliced	1
1/4 cup	frozen corn kernels	60 mL
1/2- 1 cup	shredded pizza cheese OR Cheddar and mozzarella combined	125-250 mL

- Preheat oven to 375°F (190°C). Place tortillas on a cookie sheet.

- Spread with refried beans and top with salsa, tomato, corn and cheese. **Don't overload, remember, less is better.**

- Bake for 12-15 minutes, until cheese is melted and tortillas and cheese are beginning to brown.

Variations

POTATO PIZZA – Sauté sliced **cooked potato**, sliced **onion** and dried **rosemary** in olive oil for about 8-10 minutes. Spread over **tortilla or pizza base**; top with grated **mozzarella cheese**. Bake as on page 100.

PEAR PIZZA – Try it – it's light and delicious. Arrange thin slices of Bartlett **pears** on **tortilla or pizza base**. Sprinkle with crumbled **blue cheese or** thin slices of **Brie** and a few **red pepper flakes**. Bake as on page 100.

Cook's Tips

For a little more "heat" add 1/4 tsp. (1 mL) **Tabasco or hot sauce** to the salsa.

The remaining refried beans can be used in a fajita, or added to any minestrone or vegetable soup.

SUPER-QUICK QUESADILLAS

Fill and fold a tortilla to make a quesadilla (a Tex-Mex grilled cheese sandwich). Quesadillas are my favorite quick-to-make-and-eat lunch or snack standbys. Eaten with a bowl of soup or a salad and a fruit dessert they are a full meal.

To assemble Quesadillas

- Heat a large, non-stick frying pan over medium-high heat.
- Lay a 10″ (25 cm) tortilla on the counter. Cover half with filling. Fold the uncovered half over the filling. Transfer to the frying pan and cook until golden, turning once, about 2 minutes per side.

CHEESE QUESADILLA – Spread half the **tortilla** with **processed cheese spread**; sprinkle with ¹/₂ cup (125 mL) grated **mozzarella cheese**. Fold and cook as above.

ITALIAN QUESADILLA – Spread half the **tortilla** with **chunky pasta sauce**. Top with a few slices of **salami** cut in strips, ¹/₂ tsp. (2 mL) **basil** and ¹/₂ cup (125 mL) grated **cheese**. Fold and cook as above.

CHICKEN OR HAM SWISS QUESADILLA – Cover half the **tortilla** with **creamy mustard**, 1 slice of **deli chicken or ham** cut in strips and ¹/₂ cup (125 mL) grated **Swiss cheese**. Fold and cook as above.

TEX-MEX QUESADILLA – Spread half the **tortilla** with **refried beans**. Top with grated **cheese**, a little chopped **jalapeño** and chopped **green onion**. Fold and cook as above.

TOMATO, FETA AND PESTO QUESADILLA – Crumble 4 oz. (115 g) of **feta cheese**; add 2 **Roma tomatoes**, chopped, 1 tbsp. (15 mL) of sliced **black olives** and 1 tbsp. (15 mL) of **pesto**. Mix and spread on half of a 10″ (25 cm) **tortilla**. Fold and cook as above.

CHILI AND CHEDDAR QUESADILLA (leftover or canned) – Allow about ¹/₂ cup (125 mL) **chili** for half of a **tortilla**. Sprinkle with **Cheddar** and chopped **jalapeños** if you like. Fold and cook as above.

VEGGIE QUESADILLA – Slivered **red or green peppers**, a little chopped **red onion** and **tomato**, ¹/₂ cup (125 mL) grated **cheese**. Fold and cook as above.

TUNA QUESADILLA – Try drained chopped **tuna**, 3¹/₂ oz. (106 g) can, a little **mayo**, chopped **celery or green onion** and grated **Cheddar cheese**. Fold and cook as above.

Fajitas – Chicken

Fajitas are like stir-fries, fast, easy and great tasting. Some people eat them with a knife and fork. I think they taste even better when eaten hot-dog style.

2 tsp.	vegetable oil	10 mL
2	boneless, skinless chicken thighs or a small chicken breast cut into 1″ (2.5 cm) wide strips	2
1 cup	combined, chopped onion and green or red pepper	250 mL
1 tsp.	chili powder	5 mL
pinch	cumin powder	pinch
squirt	lime juice OR lemon juice	squirt
	salt and pepper to taste	
2, 8″	flour tortillas	2, 20 cm

Fajita Toppings
diced tomato, a little grated Cheddar cheese,
salsa, sour cream OR yogurt

- Heat oil in a medium-sized non-stick skillet over medium-high heat. Add chicken; stir and cook for 1-2 minutes; add onion and peppers. Stir and cook until chicken is almost done, about 5 minutes. Sprinkle with chili powder, cumin, lime juice, salt and pepper. Stir and cook for 1-2 minutes.

- **To build your fajita**: spread the middle of each warmed tortilla with a little grated cheese; add some chicken mixture, a little tomato, salsa and sour cream. Fold up the bottom half; fold one side over, then roll. The fajitas are ready to serve.

Pictured on the front cover

Variations

BEEF FAJITAS – Substitute 4 oz. (115 g) **beef steak**, thinly sliced, for the chicken. Sprinkle beef with a pinch of **red pepper flakes**.

Replace chili powder and cumin with 1-2 tsp. (5-10 mL) **fajita or taco seasoning**.

Cook's Tips

Tortillas are tastier and easier to roll when you heat them a little. Heat in a medium-hot skillet. Put 2 on the pan, for 2 minutes; turn over and continue heating, about 2 minutes. OR place 3 or 4 tortillas on a microwave-safe plate, cover with a paper towel and microwave on HIGH for 1 minute or heat, covered in a 350°F (180°C) oven for a few minutes.

Leftovers, without sour cream, can be rolled into a tortilla, wrapped in plastic wrap, stored in the fridge and reheated in a microwave.

Vegetable Burrito

Think of this as a New Mexico stir-fry in a tortilla. The recipe makes 2 large burritos bursting with flavor and goodness. Have 1 for your meal. Save the second . . . or eat it now.

2 tsp.	vegetable oil	10 mL
2 cups	chopped vegetables, choose from onions, red, green and yellow peppers, small zucchini, tomatoes, broccoli or cauliflower florets, corn niblets, frozen or canned	500 mL
1 tbsp.	tomato paste	15 mL
1 tsp.	chili powder	5 mL
1/2, 14 oz.	can black beans, rinsed and drained	1/2, 398 mL
1 tbsp.	chopped fresh cilantro leaves or 1/2 tsp. (2 mL) dried cilantro	15 mL
1 cup	shredded mozzarella, Cheddar OR Monterey Jack cheese	250 mL
2, 9"	flour tortillas	2, 23 cm
1/2 cup	medium salsa	125 mL

- Heat a large non-stick skillet over medium heat. Add oil and vegetables, tomato paste and chili powder. Stir and cook for 4-5 minutes. Add beans. Stir and cook until beans are heated through, 4-5 minutes. Using a fork, mash the beans a little.

- Meanwhile, grate cheese (onto a piece of waxed paper for easy clean up) and heat the broiler.

- Lay 2 warmed tortillas flat and divide the vegetables between them, making a sausage shape just below the center. Sprinkle with half the cheese.

- Fold the tortilla envelope style – bottom up, sides in, top down and place in a lightly greased ovenproof dish, seam side down. Spread with salsa and sprinkle with remaining cheese. Place under the broiler until the cheese melts and is bubbly.

Toaster Oven Method

Place the burritos on the toaster oven tray. Heat with the oven at broil.

Variations

DELUXE BURRITO – Serve with **sour cream and guacamole**.

BREAKFAST BURRITO – Fill warmed **tortillas** with hot scrambled **eggs**, sautéed **onions** and **hash brown potatoes**. Fold as above. No need to bake. Serve with **salsa**.

CHILI BURRITO – Fill warmed **tortillas** with leftover **chili**. Fold and bake as above with **cheese** and **salsa** inside and out. Serve with **salsa**.

BEAN BURRITO – Heat 1/2 of a 14 oz. (398 mL) can of **refried beans**. Fill warmed **tortilla** with beans. Top with chopped **tomato or salsa**. Fold and bake as above.

FISH, SEAFOOD, CHICKEN, PORK & BEEF – MAIN DISHES

SHOPPING FOR MEAT & POULTRY

It is sometimes frustrating for a single to shop the meat counter at the supermarket. Most of the packages are 16 oz. (500 g) or contain 2 chicken breasts, 2 pork chops, a large serving of beef, or 10-14 oz. (300-400 g) of pork tenderloin.

Here is one way to cope with larger packages of meat.

Buy the pack and think of 2 or 3 meals, repackaging when you get home, or cook the whole amount and divide and repackage for future meals.

The practical alternative, of course, is to ask the butchers to break down the package, which they will do, or shop at the smaller independent meat shops in your neighborhood and buy the amount you need.

When storing my purchase for later use, I like to **divide the package into 2 or 3 portions**, place the meat in small freezer bags and keep the small bags in a large self-sealing freezer bag in the freezer. The same method is good for cooked food. The small bags can be defrosted in the fridge or in the microwave when you are short of time.

All the day-to-day meals that I prepare are ready in 15-30 minutes because that is about the amount of time that I have and that I choose to spend preparing a meal.

Cooking quickly does not sacrifice flavor or goodness. This book is designed to present quickly prepared, great-tasting dishes. These meals are low-fat, quick and easy, economical, and use ingredients on hand or easily shopped for.

PROTEIN CHOICES

We need protein for good health. Protein keeps our bodies strong, maintains muscles, aids digestion and helps our brains function. Meat, poultry, fish, eggs, dairy and soy products are our major protein sources. Grains, legumes, beans, nuts and seeds, when eaten in combination (such as trail mix or baked beans with whole-grain toast) become complete proteins. This is valuable information when you realize the popularity of peanut butter sandwiches and beans and toast.

Eating a variety of healthy foods from the grain, meat and dairy food categories provides generous amounts of valuable protein.

Fish is also low in fat and quick to prepare. Frozen fish is very good in quality as it is usually frozen within a few hours of being caught. When using fresh fish, find out when it is delivered to your market; purchase and use the same day or the next day.

Beef and **pork** are part of many of our favorite dishes. To be healthwise, plan on 3-4 oz. (85-115 g), about the size of a computer mouse, per serving per person. Choose lean cuts such as top sirloin, tenderloin chops and lean ground meats. Choosing these cuts means an increase in the cost per ounce, but not for the meal, as there is less waste.

Eggs are quick and they add protein, vitamins and minerals to our meals.

Beans, **peas**, **lentils** and **grains** have been food staples for thousands of years. We use them in starters, soups, salads and main dishes. They are inexpensive, store well, cook easily and combine with most foods. They are loaded with nutrition, are fat free and have abundant soluble fiber. For convenience, buy cooked, canned beans and lentils.

Soy beans and soy products – Soy is one of the healthiest foods available. Called "the super food," it is an almost complete protein. Using soy milk on our cereal, tofu in our stir-fries, ground soy in our meat sauces and snacking on dried roasted soy beans are some of the ways to include soy in our diets.

MEAT SAFETY

- Read the labels on meats and buy the most recently packaged.

- Refrigerate meat as soon after purchasing as possible. Place meat packages on a plate to catch any leaking juices. Use within 2 days.

- Thaw frozen meat in the refrigerator. Marinate in the refrigerator. If you marinate at room temperature do so for only 15-20 minutes before cooking. Wash the plate or bowl immediately.

- Wash cutting boards or utensils with hot soapy water. Rinse. Stand boards upright to drain and dry.

- Use separate plates and utensils for uncooked and cooked meats. When reusing the same plates and utensils, first wash thoroughly in hot soapy water.

- Use hot soapy water to immediately wash all surfaces that come into contact with raw poultry. Knives, utensils and hands, too! When the cleanup is complete, rinse out the cloth and put it into the laundry. Hang it over the edge of the basket to dry – otherwise it will stay moist and provide a home for bacteria growth.

QUICK DEFROSTING TIPS

Store meats in suitably sized amounts in the freezer. Leaving them in the store wrappings is fine. Store smaller amounts in freezer-quality wrapping.

To defrost quickly when you are desperate for meat for dinner, run hot water over the package for about 30 seconds. Remove the plastic wrap and pry off the bottom tray.

Put the meat on a microwave-safe dish and microwave for 2-3 minutes on HIGH. The meat will be thawed enough to transfer to a pan and begin browning. This works for ground meat, chicken breasts and thighs, chops and cuts up to $1/2"$ (1.3 cm) thick. This method also thaws precooked meats and rice.

Newer microwaves have efficient defrost cycles. Programmed to defrost gently, they are a true asset to quick cooks.

TEMPERATURE CHART

Using an instant-read thermometer is the best assurance for properly cooked meat. They are inexpensive and easy to use.

MEATS	TEMPERATURE
POULTRY Dark meat – thighs and drumsticks	180°F (83°C)
POULTRY Breasts and roasts	170°F (77°C)
PORK Steaks, roasts, chops, ground	160°F (71°C)
BEEF, LAMB, VEAL AND TURKEY Ground	to at least 160°F (71°C)
BEEF, LAMB AND VEAL Steak, roasts, chops (medium rare)	145°F (63°C)

Cook's Tips

Larger cuts of meat continue to cook to the inside after they are removed from the heat. Expect a rise of 10-20°F (5-10°C) as they stand.

Therefore, cook roasts and large steaks to 10°F (5°C) less than stated. Roasts removed from the oven to "stand" should be covered with a piece of foil (shiny side in to reflect heat toward roast). A pot lid or turned-over bowl can be used to cover smaller amounts.

Allow 10 minutes or more resting time for thick steaks and roasts before cutting. This enables the juices to settle. The meat will retain its moisture and be at its most tender.

F I S H &
S E A F O O D

*F*ish is loaded with protein and is relatively low in calories.

If you are very fortunate, you can buy fresh fish at a market near you. Bring it home; pan-fry in butter or oil and enjoy.

Many of us choose frozen fish because we must, and because it is convenient. Most frozen fish fillets come individually frozen and wrapped. The pieces thaw and cook very quickly. I prefer to buy real fish – the fish with no breading, coatings or stuffings. For best cooking results, follow the package directions. Add a veggie and rice or potato and your meal is ready.

CANNED FISH

1 or 2 cans of water-packed tuna, salmon, shrimp or clams on the shelf means a good meal at any time. A $7^1/_2$ oz. (213 mL) can of drained salmon or tuna will make 2 regular servings or 1 very generous serving.

TUNA AND SALMON, look for:

Tuna and Mushroom Frittata, page 35

Tuna or Salmon Sandwich, page 39

Seafood Wrap, page 40

Tuna Melt, page 44

Tuna or Salmon Spread, page 48

Cobb Salad, page 70

Salade Niçoise, page 71

Tuna or Salmon Salad, page 71

Curried Tuna Salad, page 72

Pasta with Tuna and Garlic, page 95

Salmon Puff, page 113

Drained, mashed **sardines** spread on toasted **whole-wheat bread** and topped with **ketchup or bread and butter pickles** is also good.

SHRIMP

Add drained canned **shrimp** to a **tossed green salad** OR a salad with **seasonal fruit** and **greens**.

Canned shrimp makes a delicious, nutritious **Seafood Omelet**, page 33, **sandwich**, pages 39 and 44, or **starter**, page 48, OR toss with **lemon juice** for a great topping for a tossed green salad, OR add to Clam Chowder, pages 54 and 57, to make a **Seafood Chowder**.

Sprinkle drained, canned shrimp with **cajun spice or chili powder** and sauté for 2-3 minutes. Sprinkle over **Caesar Salad**, page 60, for a Cajun Shrimp Caesar.

Fish Fillets With Cheese Croûtons

A crunchy, cheesy topping and tender flaky fish.

	vegetable oil to grease baking pan	
1 or 2	cod fillets	1 or 2
1/4 cup	milk	60 mL
	salt and pepper to taste	
1 tsp.	lemon juice	5 mL
1	slice whole-wheat OR white bread, crusts removed	1
2-3 tbsp.	grated Cheddar cheese	30-45 mL

- Preheat oven to 375°F (240°C). Oil a gratin dish or top of a small casserole.

- Place fish in dish and pour milk over. Sprinkle with salt, pepper and lemon juice. Cut bread into 1/2" (1.3 cm) cubes. Place bread cubes on fish and sprinkle with grated cheese.

- Bake for 15-20 minutes, until fish flakes easily with a fork, bread cubes are crispy and cheese is melted.

Variations

BAKED SALMON – Place a salmon steak or fillet in an oiled dish and spread with a mixture of 2 tbsp. (30 mL) **mayo**, a squirt of **lemon juice**, a little grated **lemon peel** and a pinch of dried **dill**. Bake as above.

Salmon Steak

A hint of lime and ginger brings a taste of Thai to this easy salmon dish.

1 tbsp.	fresh squeezed lime juice	15 mL
1 tsp.	honey	5 mL
1 tsp.	freshly grated ginger OR a sprinkle of dried ginger	5 mL
	salt	
1	salmon steak	1
2 tsp.	vegetable oil	10 mL

- Rub lime juice, honey, ginger and salt into both sides of fish.

- Heat a non-stick skillet over medium-high heat. Add oil. Place salmon in skillet and cook until lightly browned, 3-4 minutes. Turn over and cook 3-4 minutes more, until fish is cooked through. Reduce heat and lift pan from element if the fish begins to smoke.

GO WITHS – Rice and cooked broccoli or a green salad with tomatoes.

Cook's Tips

When cooking fish, the baking dish must be only slightly larger than the fish as the milk poaches the fish and keeps it moist.

To test for doneness, cut into fish with a fork. The fish is done when it flakes easily.

Sole Almondine

This recipe is one of my favorite fish dishes. Baked in the oven, there is no fuss, no mess and it can be easily expanded when you are joined by a friend.

1 or 2	fish fillets – sole, orange roughy OR pickerel	1 or 2
2 tbsp.	sliced almonds	30 mL
1 tbsp.	butter OR margarine, softened	15 mL
2 tsp.	grated lemon peel	10 mL
	salt and pepper	
	a generous squeeze of fresh lemon juice	

- Preheat oven to 375°F (190°C).
- Lightly oil baking dish. Place fish in oiled pan.
- Combine almonds, butter and lemon peel in a small dish. Spread over fish. Sprinkle with salt and pepper. Squeeze lemon juice over top
- Bake, uncovered, about 15 minutes. The fish is done when it flakes easily.

Cucumber Sauce

Serve this light, refreshing sauce with fish dishes, fish burgers and curries.

1/4 cup	reduced fat yogurt OR sour cream	60 mL
2 tbsp.	mayonnaise OR creamy cucumber salad dressing	30
pinch	EACH dried dill, parsley and salt	pinch
1/4-1/2 cup	peeled, seeded, diced cucumber	60-125 mL

- Combine all ingredients. Refrigerate until needed.

Makes about 3/4 cup (175 mL)

Tuna Burger

These are tasty and quickly made from your pantry stock.

6 1/2 oz.	can water packed tuna, drained	184 g
1	egg	1
1/4 cup	fine bread OR cracker crumbs	60 mL
1/4 cup	yogurt OR mayonnaise	60 mL
1 tsp.	curry powder	5 mL
	salt and pepper	

- In a small bowl, flake tuna; mix with remaining ingredients. Shape into 2-3 patties.
- Cook in a non-stick pan over medium heat until hot and lightly browned.
- Serve in a bun with lettuce, tomato and cucumber slices, and a little mayo or chutney.

Serves 2-3

Variations

Also try canned salmon. Leftovers may be diced or crumbled and added to a salad or mixed with a little mayo for a sandwich filling. Add a slice of tomato and lettuce.

Salmon Puff

Use a microwave-safe casserole for this quick flavorful fish dish. Serve with Cucumber Sauce, page 11, or a commercial tartar sauce.

7¹/₂ oz.	can sockeye salmon, undrained	225 g
4	soda crackers, crushed	4
1	egg, beaten with a fork or small whisk	1
1 tsp.	lemon juice	5 mL
¹/₂ tsp.	dried dillweed	2 mL
	salt and pepper to taste	
¹/₄ tsp.	hot pepper sauce	1 mL

- Spoon salmon into a small bowl. Crush the bones with a fork. Add crackers, egg, milk, dill and a sprinkle of salt and pepper. Mix well.

- Pour into a lightly oiled 2-cup (500 mL) casserole. Cover with waxed paper or matching lid. Microwave on HIGH for 3-5 minutes, or until salmon mixture puffs up and begins to set. Do NOT overcook. Set aside to cool.

GO WITHS – Lemony couscous and a green salad with tomatoes.

Spicy Garlic Shrimp

Bags of frozen shrimp are available in the frozen food section at the supermarket. Put the rice on to cook, then heat a little oil in a non-stick pan, add garlic, shrimp and a little seasoning, cook and serve over rice.

2 tsp.	vegetable oil	10 mL
4-6 oz.	frozen shrimp, thawed and patted dry with a paper towel	115-200 g
1	small garlic clove, minced or ¹/₂ tsp. (1 mL) minced garlic in a jar	1
¹/₂ cup	orange juice	125 mL
¹/₄ tsp.	hot pepper sauce	1 mL
¹/₂ tsp.	Worcestershire sauce	2 mL
pinch	brown sugar	pinch
	sprinkle of salt	

- Assemble all ingredients before you begin, this cooks quickly.

- Heat oil in a medium, non-stick pan over medium-high heat. Add shrimp and garlic. Cook and stir for about 2 minutes.

- Add orange juice, pepper sauce, Worcestershire sauce, sugar and salt. Cook and stir gently, about 3 minutes more, until shrimp are heated through and sauce is reduced a little. Serve over rice.

C H I C K E N

Choose boneless, skinless pieces for quick-cooking convenience. I use breast when I want the appearance of the white meat in salads or creamy sauces.

Thighs are more flavorful and less expensive than breasts. They are a good choice when making tomato-sauced and/or stewed dishes.

Chicken cooks quickly: sauté, stir-fry, broil or bake. Overcooking causes chicken to loose its juices and dry out, resulting in tough meat. Use a medium heat setting and cook until fork tender.

Chicken breasts are moist and flavorful when marinated and oven-cooked. Marinate for 6-24 hours. When you are short of time, marinate for at least half an hour. Remember, your favorite oil and vinegar-based salad dressing makes an instant marinade.

In 10 minutes or so of cooking time chicken is ready to serve

Remember to discard marinade.

POULTRY

Poultry is versatile. Its mild flavor invites herbs, spices and sauces. Serve it hot in a stew or a curry, cold in a sandwich or for a picnic supper. The leftovers become part of a quesadilla or a salad.

When the skin is removed, poultry is the leanest animal protein available. Try boneless skinless turkey or chicken breast, chicken thighs and ground turkey. **Ground chicken and turkey can replace ground beef in most recipes**. One breast or 2 thighs may be enough for a meal. You may choose to cook more than 1 serving. Think about tomorrow's evening meal or lunch at work, and make a chicken salad or sandwich to go.

Here are the simplest ways to prepare this versatile staple. Use chicken or turkey to make a salad, top a salad or as the main ingredient in a casserole. Sauced chicken takes on the flavors of France, Italy, Mexico and more.

Chicken – How to Quick-Cook

Choose chicken breasts or thighs, bone in or out.

Stove-Top Method

- Heat 2 tsp. (10 mL) **vegetable oil** in a medium non-stick skillet over medium-high heat. Add **chicken pieces**, sprinkle with **salt** and **pepper** and brown on both sides. Reduce heat and cook for 8-12 minutes. Bone-in pieces take slightly longer to cook. Use the same method for bite-sized pieces and chicken strips. Pieces will cook in about 5 minutes and strips in 3 minutes. Chicken is cooked when springy to the touch and no pink juices remain.

- Cooked chicken pieces are ready to eat with a salad or to be sauced for a main dish. Strips can top a salad or fill a pita or bunwich.

Chicken – How to Quick-Cook *continued*

Oven Method

- Bake 1, 2 or 4 chicken breast halves or 2, 4 or 6 thighs. Heat oven to 375°F (190°C).

- Place chicken on a lightly oiled shallow pan (1 or 2 pieces of chicken can be baked in a shallow casserole top). Brush chicken pieces, with 1 of the following:

Marinade Suggestions

Commercial **Teriyaki Sauce or Sweet and Sour Sauce**

1-2 tbsp. (15-30 mL) commercial **salad dressing**: Italian, balsamic, vinaigrette, herb, sun-dried tomato, etc.

A little **vegetable oil** and **hoisin sauce or salsa**

Vegetable oil, **salt**, **pepper** and **Mrs. Dash Original Seasoning**

- Cook for 30-40 minutes, basting the chicken twice as it cooks. Bone-in chicken takes slightly longer to cook.

Chicken Nuggets – Low-Fat

Heat oven to 400°F (200°C). Cut a boneless, skinless **chicken breast** into about 6 pieces (cut as many breasts as you need). Dip pieces into a small bowl of **water**, **milk**, **low-fat mayo or salad dressing**. Then dip into a small bowl of **Shake and Bake Coating Mix or bread or cracker crumbs**. Place on a lightly greased baking pan (or line pan with foil). Bake for 12-15 minutes. Serve with **mango chutney or your favorite dipping sauce**.

Pan-Cooked Chicken Breasts

A cooked chicken breast can become a chicken bunwich, diced into a chicken salad or soup, sliced to top a green salad or cubed and used in recipes listing cooked chicken as an ingredient.

1 or 2	boneless, skinless chicken breast halves	1 or 2
1/2 tsp.	dried Italian herbs OR basil	2 mL
	salt and pepper to taste	
1 tbsp.	vegetable oil	15 mL

- Place chicken between 2 pieces of waxed paper and flatten slightly with a pot bottom or small plate. Rub chicken with Italian herbs, salt and pepper.

- Heat oil in a non-stick skillet over medium heat. Add chicken and cook about 4 minutes per side, until lightly browned and cooked through.

Cook's Tip

Chicken is cooked when juices run clear when the breast or thigh is pierced with a fork.

SUPER-QUICK CHICKEN

Quickly cooked chicken breasts and thighs are meal savers.

One-Pot Chicken and Vegetables

- **Cook** 1 boneless, skinless **chicken breast or** 2 or 3 boneless, skinless **thighs**, cut into bite-sized pieces, in a lightly oiled skillet over medium-high heat for 3 or 4 minutes.

- **Add** a little thinly sliced **onion** and **celery**, a small **potato**, cut into 1" (2.5 cm) pieces, and 1 cup (250 mL) of fresh or frozen **broccoli florets**. Sprinkle with **salt** and **pepper** and a dash of **garlic powder**, if you like.

- **Stir in** 1 single-serving can of **mushroom or chicken soup**. Bring to a boil, cover, reduce heat and cook until vegetables are tender.

- A slosh of **white wine or** a generous squirt of **lemon juice** gives this dish a flavor punch!

Chicken Curry

- **Cook** 1 boneless, skinless **chicken breast** or 2 or 3 boneless, skinless thighs, cut into bite-sized pieces, in a lightly oiled skillet over medium-high heat for 3 or 4 minutes. Sprinkle with **salt** and **pepper**, 1 tsp./5 mL (more or less) **curry powder** and a pinch EACH of ground **cumin** and **cinnamon**.

- **Add** a small **potato**, cut into bite-sized pieces, $1/2$ an apple, diced, and a few **raisins** or chopped **apricot** halves.

- **Stir in** 1 can ready-to-serve **cream of chicken soup** or $3/4$ cup (175 mL) **chicken broth or water**. Bring to a boil; reduce heat; cover and simmer until flavors are blended and chicken is cooked, about 5 minutes.

- The pleasure of eating curries is enhanced when you serve them with **condiments**. Try a mixture of sweet, savory and salty . . . a little chopped **banana or orange**, chopped **green or red onion**, chopped **peanuts** and a 1-2 spoonfuls of **mango chutney**.

Chicken Fajita – *My quickest, most favorite meal!*

- **Cut** a boneless, skinless **chicken breast** into $1/2$" (1.3 cm) strips.

- **Prepare** about 2 cups (500 mL) of chopped **veggies**. Choose **onions**, **red peppers** and **green peppers** and 1-2 **garlic clove**s.

- **Heat** a non-stick skillet over medium-high heat. Add a little **oil**, chicken and veggies, cook and stir for a few minutes, until chicken browns a little and changes color.

- **Sprinkle** with **chili powder**, a pinch of **cumin** and a generous squeeze of **lime or lemon juice** (I like lime best.) Stir a couple of times.

- **Spoon** onto 2 warmed large **tortillas**. Add a generous amount of grated **Cheddar cheese**. Roll and serve with **salsa** and **sour cream**.

Sweet and Sour Chicken

Super-quick because there is no need to brown the chicken first. Make the sauce; add the chicken and vegetables; cook a little and serve. It looks good and tastes great.

Sweet and Sour Sauce

4 oz.	single serving can unsweetened pineapple tidbits or pineapple pieces cut in half, drained – juice used in sauce	113 mL
1 tbsp.	white vinegar	15 mL
1 tsp.	honey OR sugar	5 mL
1 tsp.	soy sauce	5 mL
1 cup	chicken broth OR water	250 mL
pinch	ground ginger	pinch
1	boneless, skinless chicken breast (1 half)	1
1/2	small onion, thinly sliced	1/2
1	celery stalk, thinly sliced	1
1/2	green pepper, seeded, sliced	1/2
2 tsp.	cornstarch	10 mL
2 tbsp.	water OR chicken broth	30 mL
	salt and pepper to taste	

- **To make the Sweet and Sour sauce**, combine juice drained from pineapple, vinegar, honey, soy sauce, broth and ginger in a small saucepan and heat.

- While sauce is heating, cut chicken into bite-sized pieces; add to sauce.

- Bring sauce to a boil. Add onion, celery and peppers. Return sauce to a boil. Reduce heat and simmer for 5 minutes. Add pineapple.

- Mix cornstarch with water in a small bowl or cup. Stir into the sauce. Bring to a boil, stirring, and cook for 1 minute, until sauce is thickened and clear. Season and serve.

GO WITHS – Long-grain white rice, basmati or brown rice to soak up the delicious sweet and sour sauce.

Cook's Tips

It is a good idea to use separate cutting boards for fresh produce and raw meats.

As a hurried cook, prepare, cut, chop and add to the pan as you go – except for stir-fries. Be sure to have all stir-fry ingredients chopped and ready before you begin to cook, otherwise the ingredients added to the pan first will be overcooked.

Sautéed Chicken Breasts with Lemon and Garlic

Lemon and garlic added to the broth make a vibrant dish of pan-cooked chicken. Cook 2 breasts, reserving the second one for another meal.

1 tbsp.	vegetable oil	15 mL
2	boneless, skinless chicken breasts (1 whole breast)	2
	flour to coat chicken	
	salt and pepper to taste	
¹/₂ cup	chicken broth OR apple juice OR a	125 mL
	combination of white wine and chicken broth	
2 tsp.	fresh lemon juice	10 mL
1	garlic clove, minced	1
1 tsp.	grated lemon zest	5 mL
2 tbsp.	dried parsley flakes or ¹/₄ cup (60 mL) chopped fresh	30 mL

- Heat a non-stick skillet over medium-high heat; add oil. Coat chicken with flour and a sprinkle of salt and pepper. Add to pan. Cook until lightly browned, 3-4 minutes per side.

- Add broth and lemon juice to 1 side of skillet; stir to blend. Bring to a boil; baste chicken. Reduce heat to low; cover and simmer for 5 minutes, until chicken is done. Baste halfway through cooking time.

- Transfer chicken to a plate and cover (a pot lid will do). Add garlic, lemon zest and parsley to the skillet. Increase heat; cook and stir about 2 minutes to combine flavors and reduce sauce. Pour sauce over chicken and serve.

Pictured opposite

Super-Quick Chicken and Tomato

Tomato soup with basil and oregano makes a quick sauce for this chicken dish.

4	boneless, skinless chicken breasts	4
	oil spray for pan	
1	tomato, sliced	1
10 oz.	can tomato with basil and oregano soup or a similar product	398 mL
	pepper to taste	

- Flatten chicken breasts, in a small plastic bag or between 2 pieces of waxed paper, with your hand or a meat mallet.

- Heat a large, non-stick skillet over medium-high heat and spray with vegetable oil. Add chicken breasts and cook for 2 minutes on each side.

- Top chicken pieces with tomato slices and add soup. Bring to a boil; reduce heat to simmer. Cover and cook for 8-10 minutes, until no pink color remains and juices run clear when the chicken is pierced with a small knife.

- Sprinkle with freshly ground pepper.

Serves 4 – **cook 2 breasts to serve 2** – the remaining ingredients are the same

MAIN COURSE – CHICKEN

Sautéed Chicken Breasts with Lemon and Garlic, page 118

Rice with Spices and Nuts, page 88

Greek Salad, page 65

Sautéed Cherry Tomatoes, page 77

Grilled Orange Soy Chicken Breasts

For convenience I have used orange juice in this marinade recipe. Save time and cook 2 chicken breasts.

Orange Soy Marinade

1/4 cup	orange juice	60 mL
1 tbsp.	soy sauce	15 mL
1	small garlic clove, shredded	1
1/4 tsp.	grated ginger root	1 mL
	salt and pepper	
2 tsp.	sesame oil (use vegetable oil if you don't want to buy sesame oil)	10 mL
1	boneless skinless chicken breast (1 half)	1
	vegetable oil or oil spray for pan	

- In a small bowl or cup, stir together juice, soy sauce, garlic, grated ginger, salt, pepper and oil. Place chicken in a bowl. Cover with marinade and plastic wrap or waxed paper. Refrigerate for at least 1/2 hour and up to 24 hours. Turn a couple of times.

- To cook, set the top rack of the oven 4-5 inches below the top heating element. Turn oven on to broil.

- Lightly coat a small shallow pan with oil. Place chicken on the pan. Brush with marinade. Brown chicken for 5 minutes. Turn and brush with marinade. Broil about 5 minutes more, or until chicken is cooked through. Discard marinade.

Stove-Top Cooking

Heat a little oil in a non-stick pan over medium heat. Cook chicken, turning once, for 10-15 minutes, or until no longer pink inside. Brush twice with marinade while cooking.

Marinade Variations

To vary the flavor and to produce a lovely glaze on the chicken, try 2 tbsp. (30 mL) **marmalade or apricot jam** in place of the orange juice.

GARLIC AND LEMON MARINADE – 2 tbsp. (30 mL) **vegetable or olive oil**, juice of 1/2 **lemon**, 1 tsp. (5 mL) grated **lemon zest**, 2 minced **garlic cloves** or 1/2 tsp. (2 mL) **garlic powder**.

Cook's Tips

When you have no time to marinate chicken; brush the breasts with oil and sprinkle with herbs or seasoning salt and pepper; bake, grill or broil.

Always keep a can of frozen lemonade and/or orange juice in the freezer. The amount you need for a glass of juice or to season a sauce or dessert can be spooned out without thawing.

Quick Chicken Curry

Savory chicken with fruit is the start of a memorable meal. Add a second piece of chicken for 2 servings.

1 tsp.	vegetable oil	5 mL
1	chicken breast (half), about 6 oz. (170 g) or 2 boneless chicken thighs cut into 3/4" (2 cm) pieces	1
1 tsp.	curry powder, more or less to taste	5 mL
1 tsp.	flour	5 mL
1/4 tsp.	cumin (optional)	1 mL
1/2 cup	apple juice OR vegetable OR chicken broth	125 mL
1/2	apple, cored and cut in 1/2" (1.3 cm) pieces	1/2
1 tbsp.	raisins	15 mL
	salt and pepper to taste	

- Heat oil in a medium, non-stick skillet over medium-high heat. Add chicken pieces; stir and cook until chicken is no longer pink, 3-5 minutes.

- Add curry powder, flour and cumin to the middle of the pan. Stir and cook for 1 minute. (I use the flat of the fork to blend.)

- Stir in juice, apple, raisins, salt and pepper.

- Bring to a boil. Reduce heat and cook until apples have softened, about 5 minutes.

1-2 servings – **for additional servings**, cook 4 chicken breasts; use 2 cups (500 mL) juice or broth and double the remaining ingredients.

GO WITHS – Rice and the condiments of your choice: choose sweet, salty, smooth and crunchy, whatever you have on hand. Try chopped **red or green onion**, sliced **banana**, **orange** sections and chopped **peanuts**. Try **onions**, **cucumber**, **mango chutney** and **coconut**. Anything goes, but always peanuts – EXCEPT – see Cook's Tip below.

Variations

Expand on the curry, add a little chopped **onion** to the pan with the chicken. Vary the fruit in the sauce. Use what you have on hand. Half a **peach or pear** or part of a small can of **peaches or pineapple**.

Cook's Tip

If serving any dish that contains peanuts or nuts to friends, check with them about allergies. **Nut allergies affect about 1% of the population and can be fatal. Peanut oil and other nut oils can also cause allergic reactions.**

Be very careful about cross contamination.

Chicken and Rice with Mushrooms

There are many versions of this casserole. It is quickly made out of on-hand convenience foods, and the flavor is real comfort food.

2 tsp.	vegetable oil	10 mL
2 cups	sliced mushrooms	500 mL
10 oz.	can cream of mushroom soup	284 mL
10 oz.	can milk	284 mL
1/2 cup	regular long-grain rice	125 mL
2-3	boneless, skinless chicken breasts cut into 3″ (8 cm) pieces	2-3
	OR 6 boneless, skinless chicken thighs	
	salt and pepper	
	sprinkle EACH of garlic powder and paprika	

- Lightly grease a 9 or 10″ (23 or 25 cm) baking pan or a 10″ (25 cm) oval casserole.

- Heat oven to 350°F (180°C).

- In a small non-stick skillet over medium heat, heat the oil and sauté the mushrooms. Set aside.

- In a small bowl, combine soup and milk, adding milk a little at a time to make a smooth sauce.

- Add rice to pan or casserole; top with half the soup mixture, chicken pieces, mushrooms and remaining soup mixture.

- Sprinkle with garlic powder and paprika. Cover with a piece of foil and bake for 45 minutes. Uncover and bake about 10 minutes longer or until no pink remains in the center of the chicken pieces. Make a small cut to check.

Serves 2-3 – add a chicken breast or 2 thighs to serve 4

GO WITHS – Broccoli Salad, page 64, would be perfect with this dish. For a quick veggie dish try Baked Tomato Halves, page 77, or Sautéed Cherry Tomatoes, page 77.

Variations

Sprinkle a little dry **onion soup powder** on the soup and chicken when you add the garlic powder and paprika.

Cook's Tip

TO COOK CHICKEN, cut 1 lb. (500 g) boneless, skinless **chicken breasts or thighs** into 1″ (2.5 cm) chunks. Cook in 1 tbsp. (15 mL) **vegetable oil** over medium-high heat until chicken is tender and no pink remains, about 5 minutes. Toss and turn chicken as it cooks.

Casserole Chicken Stew

Put all of the ingredients in a casserole in the oven. Go for a walk or read a book for an hour, slice some crusty bread and dinner is ready.

14 oz.	can stewed tomatoes – chili OR Italian style	398 mL
1/2 cup	corn kernels from a bag of frozen corn	125 mL
1/2 cup	thinly sliced carrots OR celery	125 mL
1	small onion, chopped	1
1/2, 14 oz.	can chickpeas (garbanzo beans) drained	1/2, 398 mL
1	large boneless skinless chicken breast, cut into 3/4" (2 cm) pieces	1
1 tbsp.	all-purpose flour	15 mL
	salt and pepper to taste	

- Preheat oven to 350°F (180°C).

- Crush or chop tomatoes into chunks. Combine all ingredients in an ovenproof 2-quart (2 L) casserole with a lid.

- Cover and cook for 50-60 minutes, until chicken is opaque, rather than translucent and pinkish.

Makes about 5 cups (1.25 L)

GO WITHS – Serve this stew with thick slices of crusty bread or whole-wheat rolls. If you are sharing with a friend serve the quick Apple Crisp, page 170. OR, serve with rice or pasta.

Nutrition Note

Cooked tomatoes have even more health benefits than raw tomatoes. Cooking allows the body to more easily absorb lycopene, a powerful antioxidant found in tomatoes. Lycopene has been related to a lower risk of prostate, colon, breast, stomach, lung and endometrial cancers and cardiovascular disease. Tomatoes are also rich in vitamin C and have good amounts of vitamins A and B, potassium, iron and phosphorus.

Cook's Tip

Look for the preseasoned canned stewed tomatoes. These are wonderfully flavored fresh-tasting products.

P O R K

Pork Loin Chops

Pork loin chops, quickly cooked, are tender and delicious. Serve as is, with applesauce, or make a Vegetable Herb Sauce, see below. Choose chops that are 1/2-1" (1.3-2.5 cm) thick.

1 tbsp.	vegetable oil	15 mL
1 or 2	pork loin chops at least 1/2" (1.3) thick	1 or 2
	sprinkling of pepper, dried thyme, rosemary and garlic OR a commercial meat seasoning such as Mrs. Dash Original	

- Heat oil in a non-stick skillet over medium-high heat.

- Season meat with pepper and herbs, rubbing them into the meat. Brown chops, cooking for 3-4 minutes each side.

- Reduce heat to medium and cook until chops are golden brown and cooked through, about 4 minutes per side.

Variation

VEGETABLE HERB SAUCE – Move cooked chops to a plate and cover. Reduce pan heat to medium, add 1 cup (250 mL) – combined amount – of chopped **carrots**, **onion** and **celery** to the pan. Cook until lightly browned, about 5 minutes. Add 1/2 cup (125 mL) **chicken broth or water**, 1/2 tsp. (2 mL) **rosemary**, **salt** and **pepper**. Bring to a boil; reduce heat and simmer, stirring until well combined and reduced. Serve over chops.

All cuts of pork, except spareribs, are lean or extra lean. For maximum flavor and tenderness, do not overcook. The internal temperature should be 160°F (70°C). The meat is cooked as soon as the juices run clear and the meat is still juicy and slightly pink.

Ground pork, like ground beef, should be cooked until well done.

Fruited Pork Chops

Pork and fruit are perfect partners – this dish is savory and sweet.

1 tsp.	vegetable oil	5 mL
1	boneless pork loin chop, about 1" (2.5 cm) thick	1
	salt and pepper to taste	
3	dried apricot halves, quartered	3
1/2 cup	orange OR apple juice	125 mL
pinch	EACH dried cinnamon, nutmeg and ginger	pinch

- Heat oil in a small non-stick skillet over medium-high heat. Season pork chop with salt and pepper. Brown chop on both sides.

- Place apricot pieces on chop. Combine orange juice and spices and pour over.

- Reduce heat to low. Cover chop and simmer until tender, about 12 minutes. Remove lid and baste twice with pan juices.

- Remove chop and fruit to a plate, cover with a lid. Increase heat under pan to medium-high. Boil juices to reduce. Stir. When juices have thickened a little and look translucent, pour over chop and serve.

Variations

Add halved, pitted **prunes** with the apricots.

Multiply the chops and other ingredients by the number of servings you need.

Simple Mushroom Pork Chops

- Brown 2 **pork chops** in a little **oil** over medium-high heat. Sprinkle with **Mrs. Dash seasoning or a little garlic powder**, **salt** and **pepper**.

- Combine a can of **cream of mushroom soup** with 1/2 a can of **water**. Add to the pan, covering the chops. Bring to a boil. Reduce heat to simmer. Cover and cook until chops are cooked through, about 15 minutes. For more flavor and added nutrition, cook a chopped **onion** and a few sliced **mushrooms** with the chops.

Variation

To make a 1-pan meal, sauté 1/2 chopped **onion**, a few sliced **mushrooms** and a cubed **potato** with the chops. Add the soup and simmer as above.

Confetti Rice and Pork

A colorful satisfying one-pot meal. It is also delicious made with chicken breasts or thighs.

2 tsp.	vegetable oil	10 mL
4-5 oz.	pork loin chop, cut into 1/2" (1.3 cm) pieces	115-140 g
1	small onion, chopped, about 1/2 cup (125 mL)	
1/2	red pepper, chopped	1/2
1/2	green pepper, chopped	1/2
	sprinkle of salt and pepper and cayenne	
1/2 tsp.	dried basil	2 mL
14 oz.	can diced tomatoes	398 mL
1/4 cup	instant rice	60 mL

- Heat a saucepan over medium-high heat; add oil.

- Add meat and cook until beginning to brown, 3-5 minutes; add onions and peppers. Continue to stir and cook until vegetables are lightly browned, about 5 minutes more.

- Add salt, pepper and cayenne. Stir in basil, tomatoes and rice.

- Bring to a boil; reduce heat to simmer. Cook about 3 minutes. Serve.

Serves 1 – **for 2 servings**, increase amount of meat and veggies; increase rice to 1/2 cup (125 mL) and add 1/2 cup (125 mL) **chicken broth or water**.

Variations

Substitute 1 **chicken breast or** 2 or 3 **thighs** for pork and vary your choice of vegetables. Try **celery**, **carrots or** add a few frozen **peas** for the last couple of minutes of cooking time.

LEFTOVERS – For a hearty soup, heat a can of tomato or V8 juice; add leftover meat and rice. Cook over low heat for about 5 minutes, then serve.

Cook's Tip

To keep fat content down in your cooking and on your foods, use an oil spray. To make your own, buy a pump or spray container and half fill with oil of your choice. Use to give a light coating of oil to pans, baking sheets, skillets, salad ingredients, and vegetables to be roasted or broiled.

Pork Chop with Vegetable Sauce

My mother cooked pork chops and made a little sauce in the pan. We always had potatoes and creamed corn as go withs. I still like this meal. I hope you do too. Cook 1 chop or cook 2 or 3, the method is the same.

2 tsp.	vegetable oil	10 mL
1	pork loin chop	1
	salt and pepper to taste OR Mrs. Dash Original Blend Seasoning	
1	small onion chopped	1
	a few slices of carrots and celery	
2 tsp.	flour	10 mL
1 cup	chicken broth OR water, including a slosh of white wine if you have it	250 mL

- Heat a medium non-stick skillet over medium-high heat, add oil.

- Season both sides of chop/chops with salt, pepper and Mrs. Dash; place in the skillet. Cook chop for 3-4 minutes each side, until browned. Remove to a plate and cover.

- Add onion, celery and carrot to skillet. You may have to add a little oil or butter. Cook until softened and beginning to brown, about 5 minutes.

- Reduce heat a little. Sprinkle flour over vegetables. Blend in with the back of a fork. Add broth, stirring as you add.

- Place chop back in skillet. Cover with sauce. Bring to a boil; reduce heat; cover and simmer for about 10 minutes, or until meat is heated through. Taste for seasoning.

GO WITHS – Try a baked potato and a serving of corn niblets, canned or frozen.

Variations

Add sliced **mushrooms** when you add the onion and use a single-serving can of **mushroom soup** in place of the broth.

For more sauce in the original recipe, increase the flour to 1 tbsp. (15 mL) and add ½ cup (125 mL) more of broth or water.

Season and brown the **chops**, top with a slice of **onion**, an **orange or lemon** slice, a little **ketchup or chili sauce**, 1 tsp. (5 mL) of **brown sugar**. Add ½ cup (125 mL) **water or chicken broth** to the pan, bring to a boil, reduce heat, cover and simmer about 10 minutes. The onion and lemon add flavor, and are not necessarily eaten.

Replace pork chop with 2 or 3 **chicken thighs**.

Cook's Tip

To quick-bake a potato, prick a medium-sized potato with a fork; microwave on HIGH for 2 minutes and place in the oven, with your oven meal, for about 20 minutes.

French Country Stew

Here are 3 versions of this dish. French Country Stew, Pork Fricassee and Chicken Stew try all of them. Adding the vegetables to the meat and sauce makes a one-pan meal.

2	small pork loin chops, cut into 3/4" (2 cm) cubes	2
2 tbsp.	all-purpose flour	30 mL
2 tsp.	vegetable oil	10 mL
1	small or 1/2 an onion, chopped	1
1	small potato, cubed	1
	a little thinly sliced celery and carrot	
	sliced mushrooms, if you have them	
1/2	green apple (Granny Smith) cut into 1/2" (1.3 cm) pieces	1/2
2 tbsp.	raisins	30 mL
1/2 tsp.	dried rosemary OR herbes de Provence	2 mL
1 cup	broth OR water	250 mL

- Coat pork with flour. Discard extra flour. Heat oil in a medium non-stick skillet over medium-high heat. Add pork; stir and cook until pork changes color and begins to brown, about 4 minutes.

- Add onion, potato, celery, carrot and mushrooms. Stir and cook for 3 minutes.

- Add apple and raisins. Crush rosemary or herbes de Provence with your fingers and add to stew. Add broth or water. Bring to a boil; reduce heat and simmer for a few minutes, until potato is tender, apples are softened and pork is cooked.

Serves 2 – **for company**, multiply the chops and remaining ingredients by the number of servings that you need.

Pictured on page 137

Variations

PORK FRICASSEE – Omit mushrooms and rosemary. Sauté 1 crushed **garlic clove** with the onion mixture. Add **broth or** 1 cup (250 mL) of **milk** and proceed as above. Add **salt and pepper** to taste and, if you wish, a few drops of **lemon juice**. **White wine** may also be used as part of the cooking liquid.

CHICKEN STEW – Substitute boneless **chicken thighs or breasts** for pork.

Cook's Tip

Always rinse fruits and vegetables in water immediately before eating **and** before you pare or cut them. Rough-skinned produce like melons should be scrubbed lightly with a brush before cutting or paring.

Pork Tagine

This is a flavorful North African stew. Serve it with couscous, rice or pita bread. Pork or chicken Tagine is a wonderful company or potluck dish. See page 139 for a 6-serving recipe made with chicken thighs.

2 tsp.	vegetable oil OR olive oil	10 mL
2	boneless pork chops, cut in 1/2" (1.3 cm) pieces	2
1/2	medium onion, chopped	1/2
1	garlic clove, minced or 1 tsp. (5 mL) commercial minced garlic	1
1 cup	combined, finely chopped carrots and celery	250 mL
1/4 tsp.	EACH ground cumin, cinnamon and coriander	1 mL
pinch	ground ginger	pinch
3/4 cup	water OR chicken broth	175 mL
1/4 cup	chopped dates, raisins OR prunes	60 mL
1 tsp.	lemon juice	5 mL
	toasted slivered almonds as garnish	

- In a medium non-stick skillet, heat oil over medium-high heat. Add pork and brown a little.

- Add onion; reduce heat to medium and cook and stir until the onions are soft and lightly browned, about 5 minutes.

- Add garlic, vegetables, spices and water. Cook and stir. Bring to a boil; add dates and lemon juice. Reduce heat to simmer. Cover and cook about 5 minutes to blend flavors.

Serves 2

GO WITHS – Couscous, see page 76, or rice. Garnish with toasted almonds and a sprinkle of grated lemon zest.

Variations

CHICKEN TAGINE – Substitute 4 boneless chicken thighs for the pork.

For added nutrition and fiber, plus another serving, add 1 cup (250 mL) of **chickpeas**.

Cook's Tip

For a **thicker sauce**, sprinkle about 1 1/2 tsp. (7 mL) of flour over the meat and vegetables when you add the spices. Stir a little to blend.

B E E F

Buying the right cut of beef for your recipe:

Oven Roasts – Less Expensive: cross rib, blade, sirloin tip or bottom sirloin, eye of round, outside or inside round, rump. **Premium**: Top sirloin, tenderloin, strip loin, wing, prime rib, rib eye.

Grilling/Barbecue Steaks – sirloin, top and bottom sirloin, strip loin, wing, rib eye, T-bone, porterhouse, tenderloin

Marinating Steaks – round, inside, outside and eye of round steaks, sirloin tip and bottom sirloin steaks, skirt and flank steak.

GROUND MEAT

Ground beef, chicken and turkey can be interchanged in most recipes. Read the labels and look for lean beef, chicken or turkey as they have less fat than regular grinds. **Depending on the recipe, you can also purchase regular ground beef, brown and drain it, then rinse off the excess fat.** The fat content will be similar to cooked, drained lean ground beef. Supermarket packets are usually sold in 1 lb. (500 g) or more packages. This is much too much for 1 serving. Buy the package and do one of the following:

- Brown the whole package in a skillet. Make a chili or meat sauce to enjoy and to store.

- Divide meat into 3 or 4 parts. Lightly form 1 part into a patty, season and make a hamburger. Wrap and freeze the remainder for a later meal – a soup, pasta sauce, fajita, lasagne or taco salad – or use 2 portions to make Meat Loaf, page 134.

- Cook the whole package in a non-stick pan until lightly browned; drain; blot with paper towel to remove most of the excess fat; cool; divide into 3 portions and spoon into 3 small self-sealing storage bags. Freeze and keep on hand for quick additions to dishes like lasagne, soup, pasta sauce, quesadillas and pizzas.

Beef is flavorful and versatile. It contains 12 essential nutrients and is an important source for iron, zinc, protein and B vitamins.

When trimmed of visible fat, all beef cuts, except for short ribs, meet the criteria of the Health Check™ program of the Heart and Stroke Foundation. However, portion control is an important consideration. 1 serving of lean beef is about the size of a computer mouse or a deck of playing cards – about 3 1/2 oz. (100 g) cooked.

The less expensive, less tender cuts – blade, cross rib or shoulder roasts – are ideal for hearty stews and soups. Simmering makes them tender and they have more flavor than the more expensive cuts.

Veggie Notes – see veggie adaptations, under ground meat variations, using ground soy on pages 132, 133, 134, 135.

SUPER-QUICK GROUND MEAT SPECIALS

Here are some tried and true meal savers. Put the skillet on to heat. Prepare and chop the ingredients and add them to the skillet as you work. **Soy-based ground beef substitute may be used in place of ground meat in the following recipes***:*

Ground Meat Ravioli

- Cook ¼ to ½ lb. (125-250 g) **ground meat** in a lightly oiled skillet over medium-high heat until meat looses its pink color.

- Add a little thinly sliced **onion** and chopped **green or red pepper** and a sprinkle of **basil or oregano**. Cook and stir for 1-2 minutes.

- Stir in a 14 oz. (398 mL) can of **ravioli**. Bring to a boil; reduce heat and cover pan. Simmer until flavors are blended and vegetables are cooked, 5 to 10 minutes.

GO WITHS – A green salad and a fruit dessert . . . cookies too!

Saucy Ground Meat

- Cook ¼ to ½ lb. (125-250 g) **ground meat** in a lightly oiled skillet over medium-high heat until meat looses its pink color. Sprinkle with **salt, pepper** and **Mrs. Dash Original seasoning**.

- Add 1 **potato,** cut in bite-sized pieces, and a little chopped **onion** and **celery,** stir and cook for 3 minutes.

- Stir in a can of ready-to-serve **mushroom soup** or ½ a 10 oz. (284 mL) can of **condensed mushroom soup** with a ¼ cup (60 mL) of **milk or water**. Bring to a boil; reduce heat; cover and cook until vegetables are tender.

Variation

Add other vegetables if you wish.

Curried Ground Meat

- Cook ¼ to ½ lb. (125-250 g) **ground meat** in a lightly oiled skillet over medium-high heat until meat looses its pink color. Sprinkle with **salt, pepper,** 1 tsp. (5 mL) **curry powder** and a pinch EACH of **cinnamon** and **cumin**.

- Add a small **potato**, diced, ½ an **apple**, diced, and a few **raisins** or a little chopped **dried apricot**.

- Stir in ½ to 1, 14 oz. (398 mL) can of diced or stewed **tomatoes**. Bring to a boil; reduce heat; cover and cook until flavors are blended and vegetables are cooked.

- This is a good place to use up leftover **chickpeas or lentils**. Drain and add to the curry. Curries are best when served with a few extras – sweet, savory and salty **condiments** like a little chopped **banana or orange**, chopped **peanuts** and 1-2 spoonfuls of **mango chutney**.

SUPER-QUICK BURGERS

Lean ground beef makes the best hamburger. A convenient choice is the frozen preformed beef and veggie patties sold in packs of 3 or 4. Keep these on hand for an almost instant burger, or they may be cut up and added to soups or pasta sauces. Cook in a lightly oiled non-stick skillet over medium-high heat until cooked through – about 2-4 minutes per side. Do not overcook.

Burger Favorites

4 ounces (115 g) of lean ground beef makes a good burger. A perfect burger is comfort food. For new flavors try some of the toppings listed here. I especially like the chutney and chopped onion version. If you prefer, heat the bun a little before stacking it.

4 oz.	lean ground beef	115 g
	salt and pepper to taste	
	sprinkle of garlic and onion powder, if you like	

- Heat a small non-stick skillet over medium-high heat.

- Gently shape beef into a patty. Lightly spray skillet with vegetable oil. Add patty and cook until medium-well done, turning once or twice. Inside of burger will have no tinge of pink but still be moist and tender.

- Choose a **whole-wheat bun**, spread half with **Dijon or American** (hot-dog) **mustard**, top with burger, an **onion** slice, a **tomato** slice, 1-2 **pickles** and the top bun half.

GO WITHS – Green salad or coleslaw, yogurt and fruit for dessert.

Burger Variations (also try with Veggie Burgers)

- Add chopped **dill**, **basil**, **oregano or parsley** to the meat.
- Add finely minced **jalapeño peppers or garlic**.
- Add **barbecue sauce, Worcestershire or soy sauce**.
- Use a **Cajun spice mixture** for seasoning.
- Form the burger **around** a piece of cheese – try **blue**, **Cheddar**, **Brie**, etc.
- **Also, try any of these burgers with ground turkey.**

Burger Toppings

- Sautéed sliced **mushrooms** and **onions** seasoned with **salt** and **pepper**
- Grated **Swiss or Cheddar cheese**. Add to meat patty when you turn it over. The cheese will melt a little or try **gouda, mozzarella, havarti, provolone cheese**.
- Chopped **onions** and **mango chutney**
- A tablespoon (15 mL) of **barbecue or teriyaki sauce**
- Crumbled **blue or feta cheese** and thinly sliced **onion** rounds
- Sliced **tomato or salsa, guacamole** and **lettuce**
- Sautéed **mushrooms or red peppers** and **onions**

Meat Loaf

Meat loaf is the #1 choice in bistros and family restaurants. That surprises me because I prefer my homemade meat loaf and I appreciate having some left to reheat or to slice cold for sandwiches. Try this one – if you like it, make it a regular in your kitchen.

8 oz.	lean or extra-lean ground beef	250 g
1	egg white (use the whole egg if you like)	1
1/4 tsp.	salt and sprinkle of pepper	1 mL
1/8 tsp.	garlic powder	0.5 mL
1/2	small onion, finely chopped	1/2
1 tsp.	Worcestershire sauce	5 mL

• Preheat oven or toaster oven to 375°F (190°C).

• In a medium bowl, combine all ingredients. Mix lightly with a spoon or your hands. Do not over mix; overmixing toughens the meat mixture.

• Form into a loaf shape and place in a gratin dish or the flat top of a small casserole or use a 3 x 6" (8 x 15 cm) mini loaf pan.

• Bake for 30-40 minutes, until browned on top and cooked through.

GO WITHS – Baked potato and corn niblets or a salad.

Moroccan Meat Sauce

This lightly spiced meat sauce has a delectable Middle Eastern flavor. **This recipe also works with ground soy.**

4 oz.	ground beef	115 g
1/2	medium onion, chopped	1/2
1	garlic clove crushed OR 1/2 tsp. (2 mL) bottled, minced	1
pinch	EACH sugar, salt, pepper, cumin, cinnamon and ground cloves	pinch
1 tsp.	Worcestershire sauce	5 mL
14 oz.	can diced tomatoes (1/2 can is okay)	398 mL
2 tbsp.	raisins	30 mL
1 tsp.	lemon juice OR vinegar	5 mL
	1 or 2 servings of cooked rice	

• Heat a medium non-stick skillet over medium heat. Add beef and onion. Increase heat a little; cook and stir, breaking up beef as it cooks. When beef begins to brown, add garlic, salt, pepper, sugar, spices and Worcestershire sauce. Combine and cook for 1-2 minutes.

• Stir in tomatoes, raisins and lemon juice. Cook and stir over medium low heat for about 5 minutes, until liquid is reduced and beef is saucy, not soupy. Serve over rice.

Variations

Add a little grated **carrot** and chopped **celery** to the pan when you add the onion. **Substitute ground chicken, turkey or pork for the beef.**

LEFTOVERS – The sauce may be added to **tomato soup** OR spooned over a baked **potato** and topped with grated **cheese** and chopped **green onion**.

One-Pot Tomato, Beef and Couscous

This is a one-pot very quick, everyday meal.

2 tsp.	vegetable oil	10 mL
1/2 lb.	boneless sirloin, cut into 3/4" (2 cm) pieces	250 g
1	small onion chopped	1
1	garlic clove, chopped (optional)	1
14 oz.	can original or garlic and herb diced tomatoes	398 mL
1/3 cup	couscous OR 1/2 cup (125 mL) instant rice	75 mL
	salt and freshly ground pepper to taste	

- Heat a nonstick skillet over medium-high heat. Add oil and beef; cook for about 2 minutes. Add onion and garlic; stir and cook until beef is browned. Stir in tomatoes and bring to a boil.

- Stir in couscous, salt and pepper. Cover; remove from heat and let stand about 5 minutes, until liquid is absorbed

Variation

Add a little chopped **green and red pepper** when you add the couscous or rice.

One-Pan, One-Serving Harvest Stew

Comfort food in a jiffy. The ingredients for this jiffy stew can be multiplied as needed.

4 oz.	lean or extra-lean ground beef OR ground soy	115 g
1/2	small onion, chopped	1/2
1/2	potato, cut in small chunks	1/2
1/2	green pepper, chopped	1/2
1/2	carrot, thinly sliced or grated	1/2
7 1/2 oz.	can tomato sauce OR 1 cup (250 mL) diced canned tomatoes	213 mL
1/2 cup	water OR broth	125 mL
	salt, pepper and garlic powder to taste	

- Heat a non-stick pan over medium-high heat. Add beef and onion. Cook and stir until meat looses its pink color.

- Add potato, green pepper, carrot, tomato sauce and water. Bring to a boil. Reduce heat; cover and simmer about 10 minutes, until vegetables are tender. Add seasonings.

GO WITHS – Crusty bread with orange and banana slices with yogurt for dessert.

Variations

ONE-PAN, ONE-SERVING CHICKEN HARVEST STEW – Substitute 2 **chicken thighs** for the ground beef.

Substitute 12 oz. (341 mL) can of **V-8 juice** for the tomato sauce and water.

Italian Steak

A packaged blade, cross rib or round steak will make 2 generous meals as the package is usually 15-16 oz. (450-550 g). For 2 meals or 2 persons, cook the whole steak.

1 tbsp.	all-purpose flour	15 mL
	salt and pepper to taste	
8 oz.	blade, cross rib or round steak	250 g
1 tsp.	vegetable oil	5 mL
1	small onion, sliced	1
14 oz.	can Italian spice stewed tomatoes	398 mL

- Rub flour, salt and pepper into both sides of steak.

- Heat a non-stick pan over high heat; add oil and brown steak on both sides.

- Push steak to side of pan; lower heat to medium and cook onion until soft.

- Top steak with onions and tomatoes. Cover and simmer for 1-2 hours, or until very tender.

GO WITHS – Mashed potatoes or couscous.

Variation

Cook a little **green and red pepper**, **celery** and sliced **carrots** with the steak.

Leftover Options

Leftovers may be reheated.

The meat may be sliced to make a sandwich.

The sauce and the meat, chopped, may be added to vegetable soup.

Cook's Tips

INTERCHANGEABLES

Vegetable oil, canola oil, safflower oil, soy bean oil, corn oil or a blend are interchangeable. Use **olive oil** when the recipe specifies it.

Red wine, distilled white and **cider vinegars** can be interchanged. Lemon juice can also be substituted for vinegar.

Oyster sauce, hoisin sauce, stir-fry sauce and **Asian black bean sauce** are similar and can be interchanged.

For thickening sauces, 1 tbsp. (15 mL) all-purpose **flour** may be replaced by 1 1/2 tsp. (7 mL) **cornstarch or** 1 tbsp. (15 mL) quick-cooking **tapioca**.

Little jars of purchased **garlic**, kept in the fridge, mean that you always have garlic ready to use. 1/2 tsp. (2 mL) bottled garlic equals 1 clove fresh garlic, or use 1/4 tsp. (1 mL) garlic powder.

ENTERTAINING – PORK

S T I R - F R Y I N G

STIR-FRY TIPS

Add the firmer vegetables, like **carrots**, **cauliflower**, **cabbage**, **onions** and sliced **broccoli stems**, to the pan first. After a couple of minutes add the softer **broccoli florets**, **mushrooms**, **peas**, **asparagus** and **zucchini**. Turn and toss until almost cooked through.

The final touch can be a sprinkle of **light soy sauce** and a squirt of **lemon juice**, a couple of tablespoons (30 mL) of bottled **stir-fry or teriyaki sauce** or a sprinkle of **5-spice powder** and a dash of **white wine or chicken broth**.

This wonderful mixture can top **Ramen noodles**, cooked or reheated **rice**, **couscous** or 1-2 slices of cubed **toast**.

STIR-FRY "MEALS-IN-MINUTES" IDEAS

To make an almost-instant, 1-pan stir-fry, follow these easy steps:

- Have everything chopped and ready before you begin.

- Heat a little **oil** in a non-stick skillet over medium-high heat.

- Add about 1 cup (250 mL) cooked or uncooked **chicken**, **pork** or **beef** cut into bite-sized pieces or thin strips. Stir and cook for 2-3 minutes before adding vegetables.

- Add 1-2 cups (250-500 mL) chopped **mixed vegetables**, fresh or frozen. Stir and cook until meat and veggies are heated through.

- Sprinkle with a little freshly ground **pepper** and **5-spice powder**.

- Serve with cooked rice, pasta or couscous OR add instant rice for a 1-pan meal.

- For a 1-pan rice dish, add $1/3$ cup (75 mL) of **instant rice** and $3/4$ cup (175 mL) **water** or low-sodium **chicken broth**. Bring to a boil, reduce heat to low, cook for 3 minutes; remove from heat and let stand for 5 minutes.

*S*tir-frying produces tender-crisp cooked vegetables and savory tidbits of meat or shellfish. For best results, use a non-stick skillet or wok and a little oil, medium-high heat and uniformly sized pieces of meat and vegetables.

As a general rule, **for 1 serving** you will need 4-7 oz. (115-200 g) of meat, **chicken, beef or pork**. Stir and cook for 2-3 minutes before adding 1-2 cups (250-500 mL) of chopped **vegetables**.

SOME STIR-FRY COMBINATIONS TO TRY:

- Boneless **chicken breast** chunks with **red** and **green pepper** strips and **broccoli or cauliflower** florets. For a little more sauce and a boost in flavor, add 1 tsp. (5 mL) each **vinegar**, low-sodium **soy sauce** and **ketchup**, a pinch of **sugar** and **dried ginger or** 1 tsp. (5 mL) grated **fresh ginger**.

- About 4 oz. (115 g) **sirloin steak** cut into ½ x 2″ (1.3x5 cm) pieces sautéed with a little crushed **garlic**, chopped **onion**, diced **peppers**, sliced **mushrooms** and 2 tbsp. (30 mL) of **stir-fry sauce**.

- **Ground meat** with chopped **onions** and **tomatoes**, sliced **carrot** and **celery**. Add ¾ cup (175 mL) **vegetable juice or pasta sauce**.

- **Pork loin** pieces with a few **apple** slices, **broccoli** florets and **onion** chunks, 1-2 squirts **lemon juice** and 1 tsp. (5 mL) low-sodium **soy sauce**.

Variations

VEGETABLE STIR-FRY – Heat 1-2 tsp. (5-10 mL) **vegetable oil** over medium-high heat in a large non-stick skillet. Add 2-3 cups (500-750 mL) of **vegetables** in uniformly cut pieces. Toss and cook until tender-crisp. Sprinkle with **salt** and **pepper,** a dash of **5-spice powder** and a sprinkle of **lemon juice**.

Chicken and Vegetable Stir-Fry

Bottled stir-fry or Thai sauce makes this a super-quick stir-fry.

2 tsp.	vegetable oil	10 mL
1	boneless, skinless chicken breast (1 half), cut into bite-sized pieces	1
2 cups	thinly sliced vegetables, such as celery, carrots, zucchini, broccoli, onion, tomato, cabbage	500 mL
2 tbsp.	apple juice OR chicken broth OR water	30 mL
2-3 tbsp.	bottled stir-fry sauce	30-45 mL

- Heat oil in a medium non-stick skillet over medium-high heat. Add chicken pieces; stir and cook until chicken is no longer pink, 4-5 minutes. Transfer chicken to a plate and cover.

- Increase heat slightly. Add vegetables. Stir and toss until tender-crisp, 2-3 minutes.

- Add chicken and juices, apple juice and stir-fry sauce. Cook and stir until heated through, 2-3 minutes. Serve with noodles or rice.

Cook's Tip

¼ tsp. (1 mL) of garlic powder is equal to 1 clove of garlic.

Ginger-Sauced Chicken Stir-Fry

This gently spiced dish is a little fancier than the stir-fries on the previous page. It serves 2 and can be multiplied as you like. Serve with rice, Chinese wheat noodles or Ramen noodles.

Soy Ginger Sauce

3 tbsp.	cider OR rice vinegar	45 mL
2 tbsp.	sugar	30 mL
1/4 cup	water	60 mL
1 tbsp.	soy sauce	15 mL
1 tsp.	cornstarch	5 mL
2 tsp.	grated ginger root	10 mL
2-3 tsp.	vegetable oil	10-15 mL
1	large skinless, boneless chicken breast (1 half) cut into	1
	1/2 x 2" (1.3 x 5 cm) strips	
1 cup	thinly sliced celery	250 mL
1 cup	thinly sliced carrots	250 mL
1/2	red bell pepper, cut into 1" (2.5 cm) pieces or 2" (5 cm) strips	1/2
1/2	medium onion, sliced	1/2
1 tsp.	minced garlic	5 mL

- **To make the sauce**, combine all ingredients in a small saucepan. Use a small whisk or a fork. Over medium-high heat, bring the mixture to a boil, stirring constantly. Cook and stir for 1 minute. The sauce will thicken and clear.

- **To cook the stir-fry**, heat a medium non-stick skillet over medium-high heat. Add a little oil and heat. Add chicken; stir and cook until no pink remains. Remove to a plate and cover (a pot lid will do).

- Reheat skillet and add a little oil. Add celery and carrots; toss and cook for 2-3 minutes. Add pepper, onion and garlic. Stir and cook for an additional 2 minutes.

- Add chicken and garlic; stir and cook until heated through. Drizzle with sauce and serve over rice or noodles.

Variations

Try various vegetables. Think about colors and textures, make it a beautiful dish. 2-3 cups (500-750 mL) is about right for 2 people. Try **broccoli, cauliflower, asparagus, mushrooms, zucchini, snow peas or** shredded **cabbage**. When you add the cooked chicken you can add wedges of **plum tomatoes, baby corn** ears, **peas,** sliced **water chestnuts or** washed **bean sprouts**.

Cook's Tips

When buying fresh ginger, look for firm, irregularly shaped roots with smooth brown skin and no soft spots. Always grate ginger finely so the flavor will be evenly distributed in your dish. I find the best way to store and use ginger is to keep it in a tightly closed plastic bag in the freezer. To use, grate the amount you need; reseal and return to freezer. No need to peel or thaw to use! Ginger will keep for 3 months or more. Also, jars of pre-minced ginger are available in most produce departments.

Chicken-Fried Rice

For a good meal in a hurry, make fried rice. It is an easy 3-step process. Make the egg strips; stir-fry the vegetables and meat; add the rice and egg.

1 tsp.	vegetable oil	5 mL
1	egg	1
1 tsp.	vegetable oil	5 mL
1 cup	assorted vegetables – sliced mushrooms, finely diced celery, sliced green onion, broccoli florets, medium grated carrots, frozen peas, green OR red pepper, diced	250 mL
$^1/_2$ cup	leftover cooked chicken, cut into small pieces	125 mL
$^1/_2$	garlic clove, minced (optional)	$^1/_2$
$^1/_2$-1 cup	cooked rice	125-250 mL
1 tsp.	soy sauce	5 mL
	sprinkling of pepper	

• Heat 1 tsp. (5 mL) oil in a small non-stick skillet over medium-high heat. Beat egg with a whisk or fork; add to pan; cook until set. Turn cooked egg out onto a plate and cover. When cool cut into strips.

• Heat 1 tsp. (5 mL) oil in a medium non-stick skillet over medium-high heat. Add vegetables, except mushrooms; cook 2-3 minutes; add mushrooms and cooked chicken. Cook and stir until heated through, about 3 minutes. Stir in garlic. Stir in soy sauce.

• Add rice and egg strips. Stir gently. Reduce heat to medium and cover for a few minutes until heated through.

Variations

No chicken! Cook the dish without and enjoy, or serve as a side dish with deli chicken.

SHRIMP-FRIED RICE – Substitute shrimp for the chicken.

To use fresh chicken, turkey or beef, cut a small piece of meat, about 3 oz. (85 g), into $^1/_2$" (1.3 cm) pieces; add to the pan; cook for 2 minutes and add the vegetables.

PORK-FRIED RICE – Omit the egg, prepare and cook 1 **pork loin chop** as in variation above. Season with **5-spice powder** and add the vegetables. Garnish with chopped **cashews**.

F O O D ,   F U N
& F R I E N D S

ENTERTAINING PLANNER

Here is a strategy that works for me:

- **Plan Ahead – Write it Down – Get Help**

- **Begin at least 2 weeks in advance** – Plan the kind of event, the time and the number of guests. Call and invite everyone.

- **Make lists** – Plan the menu, the shopping and "to do's" – advance and last minute.

- **5-7 days ahead** – Check to see what you need to buy in the way of food and supplies for the party, what needs to be cleaned and reorganized: cutlery, dishes, glasses, serving dishes, linens, candles, music, wine, canned foods and food basics.

- **2 days ahead** – Clean and tidy. Buy perishables and flowers. Check and recheck your lists.

- **1 day ahead** – Prepare food that can be refrigerated overnight. Set the table. Clean the kitchen and clear the counters and the fridge as much as possible so that you have space to work. Set out the serving dishes and utensils. Make a space for the dessert and the coffee needs. Do you have enough chairs?

- **Early on the day of the party** – Prepare all the ingredients that you will be using in your food preparation that day. For example: chop onions and store them in plastic bags; roast nuts; grate cheese; measure herbs and spices or have them at hand.

- **In the afternoon** – Check lists. Cook what you can. Tidy the kitchen; run and empty the dishwasher.

- **For final meal preparations** – Make a list with the task and approximate time:
    5:30 – Stew in oven at 350°F (180°C);
    6:00 – Rice in oven

- Put post-its on dishes as reminders – "add croûtons" or "add chopped cilantro".

- **Do a last tidy** of the living room and bathroom.

- **Relax**. It will all fall into place and everyone will have a good time.

I like impromptu gatherings best. Gatherings that just happen, with good company and good food are fun.

No-stress planning for special events – birthdays, anniversaries and holiday celebrations call for a different strategy.

Here is an outline of tasks that can arise when you entertain, and tips for getting them done with as little fuss as possible.

GETTING HELP

- As I mentioned, **get help**. What kind, depends on you. A friend may offer to bring dessert or salad. **Accept**. My husband makes a wonderful beef stew and a saucy fish dish that our friends prefer to anything I cook. Lucky me!

- For large family gatherings, my daughter comes the day ahead to help with the table and kitchen preparations. I prefer to ask one person to help clear the table between courses, put dishes in the dishwasher, put good silver cutlery in warm water in a bowl or in the sink, and help serve coffee or desserts. Leave the dishes until later.

CLEANING UP

- **Plan for cleanup** – Most importantly, clean as you prepare and cook. Tidy up, rinse out, wash, dry and put away.

- Be sure to run and empty the **dishwasher** before the meal and have the counters clear for the after-dinner dishes. NO dishwasher? **Scrape, rinse and stack** the dishes to one side of the sink.

- Always put **flatware** into a container of soapy water (a small pail or pot will do) especially if it is silver, as the food, dressings and sauces mark and tarnish the metals.

- **At the end of the evening** or gathering, load the dishwasher; wash the glassware and breakables and soak the dishes that need it. (Don't run the dishwasher while your guests are present. It doesn't contribute to the ambience.)

- When I have a good time visiting with friends and family I almost always enjoy beginning the cleanup. I put on some good music and work a little and maybe chat with a friend who has stayed to help.

Cleaning Tips

For oven spills, sprinkle salt generously on the burnt food. It reduces the smoke and makes your cleanup easier. Adding cinnamon makes the odor more pleasant.

If your oven is not self cleaning, scrape off major spills; spray oven with cleaner and let cleaner work overnight in closed oven for easier cleanup.

Put lemon or lime peels down the garbage disposal for a fresh smell.

ENTERTAINING

Menu Planning for Parties

A good meal is balanced nutritionally. A wonderful meal is planned to please the senses. Keep **COLOR**, **TEXTURE** and **FLAVOR** in mind.

Plan for a variety of **COLORS** of foods that go together. Creamy sauced chicken with confetti rice and bright green asparagus make a beautiful combination.

When planning your menu, a variety of **TEXTURES** is important, too. Think smooth and creamy, chewy, crunchy, crispy – creamy sauce, crispy salad, chewy dense bread, crunchy nuts and creamy dessert topping.

In **FLAVORS**, we like salty, sweet and spicy. The combinations of flavors we enjoy come from tradition and experience. Usually, a spicy main dish is complemented with a milder rice dish or a vegetable in season. Fresh vegetables and fruit in season are always appropriate and can be the starting point for a menu – asparagus, lots of it, with salmon and rice pilaf announces spring.

If you like a strong flavor, like garlic, use it only once in your meal. The same applies to soy sauce or ginger. **When planning a meal, think of foods and food combinations that you have enjoyed**, or take note of menus in restaurants or articles in magazines and try some of your favorites.

How many dishes is up to you. When entertaining casually, a main course with 1 or 2 sides and a salad, bread and dessert is perfect. So is a big pot of chili or stew, add crispy bread and a salad with a bakery cake or pie for dessert.

I like to think ahead a little and plan my **presentation** as well. It makes me feel good when my guests say; "Oh, that looks terrific!" or "That's beautiful!" It just means the addition of a couple of crisp lettuce leaves to one side of a white platter holding a broiled steak, sautéed mushrooms and baked tomatoes, or using chopped parsley and a little lemon zest to top a savory stew.

When **setting the table**, anything goes. Please yourself. For a while I was into smooth sea-tumbled stones and lots of candles, creamy dishes and linen napkins. One of my guests said she had never seen stones on a table before. I like the natural look very much.

Harmonize a theme through color or your cutlery, china and serving pieces. Use what you have; mix and match; borrow a piece or two; improvise and tie it all together with color, unscented candles, flowers, a cloth or decorative runner, or both. Maybe use a theme, celebratory or seasonal.

Cook's Tip

For last-minute entertaining, your local supermarket or specialty store has excellent ready-to-heat-and-serve products in the freezer or refrigerated section of the store.

FRIENDS COMING & TOO BUSY TO COOK

Supermarket Menu – Gourmet Style

When you are too busy to cook, and you have a friend or two coming to share a meal, put your trust in the supermarket or a neighborhood gourmet take-away. Try this menu or design one of your own:

Herbed Cream Cheese with Crackers; Marinated Olives or Vegetables
Lemon-Roasted Deli Chicken
Herbed Long-Grain Rice
Spring Greens with Diced Tomatoes, Croûtons and Salad Dressing
Crusty Bread and Butter
Chocolate Brownies with Ice Cream and Raspberries

- Upon arriving home, preheat oven to 200°F (93°C). Place the chicken, still in the bag, on a plate in the oven to keep warm. Put a large plate in the oven and a bowl for the rice. These will be warm when you need them.
- Put the rice on to cook and set the timer for 18 minutes.
- Place herbed cheese and olives or veggies in small bowls on a large plate or small tray – crackers on the side. Starters are ready!
- Set the table, complete with side dishes for the salad.
- Wash and dry the greens, place in a bowl. Add croûtons. Place the salad on the table, the bread and butter, too.
- Check the rice. If it is cooked, add 1 tsp. (5 mL) dried parsley and 1/2 tsp. (2 mL) dried basil. Gently mix with 2 forks. Transfer to a heated bowl and to the oven.
- Place chicken on a cutting board. Cut breast meat off in large slices. Remove legs and cut in half at the joints. Arrange chicken on heated platter. Transfer to the table or keep warm in the oven while you relax with your friends and enjoy the starters.
- For dessert, for each serving, cut a really good brownie in half and put 2 halves in each dessert dish; top with vanilla ice cream and thawed raspberries.
- Serve coffee and/or tea.

Impromptu Special – Lasagne with Friends

Recently, I enjoyed a superb impromptu meal with friends. Anna stopped at an Italian restaurant in her neighborhood and ordered a large lasagne to go. Next, she called at the bakery for a lemon meringue pie and 2 crusty baguettes. She stopped back at the restaurant for the lasagne and headed home.

At home she put the lasagne in the oven at 200°F (93°C). Her friend Leslie set the table. Anna made an enormous green salad and set it on the table with the bread, bread board and knife. Jim opened the Australian Shiraz.

Soon all the little details were in place and we were laughing and talking and feasting.

GOOD COOKING, GOOD EATING WITH GOOD FRIENDS

Here are some quick, easy and delicious entertaining favorites. The suggested menus include the page numbers for each recipe.

*

Chicken Tagine with Mango Chutney, p. 149

Rice with Spices and Nuts, p. 88

Crusty bread

Brown Sugar & Rum-Baked Bananas with Ice Cream, p. 163

*

Italian Steak, p. 136

Lemon Green Beans, p. 78

Baked Potato, p. 82

Brownie Sundae, pgs. 160, 161

*

Broccoli Salad, p. 64

Hearty Pork Stew, p. 151

Baked Potatoes with Sour Cream, p. 77

Cheesecake, purchased

*

Garden Vegetable Chili, p.156

Crispy Side Salad, p. 63

Crusty Bread

Apple Cranberry Crisp, p. 170

*

Company One-Dish Chicken, p. 150

Orange and Red Onion Salad, p. 63

Dinner Rolls

Favorite Take-Home Pastry

*

Pasta Primavera, p. 94

Thai Salad, p. 66

Crusty Bread

Fresh Strawberry Pie, p. 165

Roasted Turkey Breast

Thanksgiving and Christmas call for the tradition of turkey and all the fixings. We crave the wonderful aromas, flavors and memories of traditional family feasts.

Choose a fresh turkey breast to celebrate Thanksgiving or Christmas dinner with a friend or two. Turkey breasts are usually 1 1/2-2 lbs. (750 g-1 kg), and will provide generous servings plus a second meal or 1 or 2 sandwiches.

1/2	fresh turkey breast (1 whole side)	1/2
	salt and pepper to taste	
	Mrs. Dash Original (if you have it)	
1	small onion, quartered	1
	a few slices of carrot and celery tops	
3 tbsp.	melted butter OR margarine	45 mL
2 tbsp.	white wine, apple juice OR chicken broth	30 mL

- Preheat oven to 350°F (180°C).

- Season all sides of turkey with salt, pepper and Mrs. Dash Original. Place turkey in a small roasting plan or a suitably sized baking pan. Tuck onion, celery and carrot under the rib bones. Roast for 1 1/4 -1 1/2 hours.

- Baste with pan juices every 20 minutes. If the juices dry up, add a little more wine, juice or chicken broth and butter. Turkey is done when the internal temperature reaches 170°F (77°C). NO Thermometer? The skin will be browned and shiny; when you press the meat it will be springy, not soft, and not firm. Make a small cut with a sharp knife in the middle of the breast. The flesh should be firm, with no pink remaining. See Cook's Tips on page 109.

- Remove turkey from oven. Place turkey on a large plate or platter; cover with aluminum foil and let rest about 10 minutes before carving. Time enough to make a little Pan Gravy (see below).

Serves 3-4

Cook's Tips

PAN GRAVY – spoon or pour off fat from pan juices (drippings). Discard fat. To pan juices add 1 cup (250 mL) **water or chicken stock**; stir and bring to a simmer. To thicken gravy, in a container with a tight-fitting lid, shake 2 tbsp. (30 mL) **flour** with 1/2 cup (125 mL) of **water**. Shake until smooth and gradually stir into simmering gravy. Cook and stir until thickened, about 3 minutes. Season with **salt** and **pepper** to taste. Add 1-2 sprinkles of **thyme** and **poultry seasoning** for added flavor.

- If you buy a frozen breast, follow the package directions for thawing and cooking.

- **Leftovers?** Make Company One-Dish Chicken, page 150, using turkey instead of chicken.

Chicken Tagine

Serve this flavorful North African stew with couscous, rice or pita bread. Chicken Tagine is a wonderful company or potluck dish.

2 tbsp.	vegetable oil OR olive oil	30 mL
12	skinless chicken thighs	12
2	medium onion, chopped	2
3	garlic cloves, minced or 3 tsp. (15 mL) commercial minced garlic	3
4 cups	combined, finely chopped carrots and celery	1 L
1 tsp.	EACH ground cumin, cinnamon and coriander	5 mL
½ tsp.	ground ginger	2 mL
2½ cups	water OR chicken broth	625 mL
1 cup	chopped dates, raisins OR prunes	250 mL
2 tbsp.	lemon juice	30 mL
	toasted slivered almonds and grated lemon zest as garnish	

- In a Dutch oven or large pot, heat 1 tbsp. (15 mL) oil over medium-high heat. Add chicken and brown a little. Remove chicken to a plate and keep warm.

- Add onion and remaining oil; reduce heat to medium. Cook and stir until onions are soft and lightly browned, about 5 minutes. Add chicken and accumulated juices.

- Add garlic, vegetables, spices and water. Cook and stir. Bring to a boil. Add dates and lemon juice; reduce heat to simmer. Cover and cook until chicken is tender and flavors are blended, about 30 minutes.

Serves 4-6

GO WITHS – Couscous, see page 76, or **rice**. Garnish with toasted **almonds** and a sprinkle of grated **lemon zest**.

Variations

1-2 cups (250-500 mL) **chickpeas** are a welcome addition.

Cook's Tip

For a thicker sauce, sprinkle about a tbsp. (15 mL) of **flour** over meat and vegetables when you add spices. Stir a little to blend. Add **water or broth**.

Company One-Dish Chicken

Assembled in minutes, this dish is a good choice for leftover chicken or turkey. The curry adds just a hint of flavor. To prepare from fresh chicken, cook as directed in the Cook's Tip below.

2-3 cups	cubed, cooked chicken OR turkey	500-750 mL
1 lb.	pkg. frozen California-style vegetables, thawed and chopped	500 g

Curried Cheddar Sauce

10 oz.	can cream of chicken soup	284 mL
1/2 cup	milk OR cream	125 mL
1 tsp.	curry powder	5 mL
1/4 cup	apple juice OR white wine	60 mL
1 cup	grated Cheddar cheese	250 mL

- Preheat oven to 375°F (190°C).

- Combine chicken and thawed vegetables in a 2½-quart (2.5 L) ovenproof casserole.

- **To make the sauce**, combine soup, milk, curry and juice in a microwave-safe glass bowl. Cook on HIGH until heated through, about 5 minutes. Stir twice.

- Add sauce to chicken and vegetables in casserole.

- Top with grated cheese and bake for 15-20 minutes, until cheese is melted and sauce is bubbly and heated through.

Serves 4

GO WITHS – Rice or serve over split hot biscuits OR croissants

Variations

Use a combination of **chopped fresh vegetables** to equal 3-4 cups (750 mL-1 L) – try **broccoli, cauliflower, carrots, onion, celery, red and green peppers** – or whatever you have on hand.

Golden Mushroom, Broccoli Cheddar and **Cream of Chicken soups** can be used for a flavor change, or, try **Cream of Asparagus soup** and add fresh or drained, canned **asparagus**.

GO WITHS – Oven-Baked Potatoes, page 82, and Baked Tomato Halves, page 77.

Cook's Tips

To cook chicken, cut 1 lb. (500 g) boneless, skinless **chicken breasts or thighs** into 1" (2.5 cm) chunks. Cook in 1 tbsp. (15 mL) **vegetable oil** over medium-high heat until chicken is tender and no pink remains, about 5 minutes. Toss and turn chicken while it cooks.

Hearty Pork Stew

A slow simmer in the oven or slow cooker blends the flavors of this hearty stew. For 4 servings, cook 1 lb. (500 g) meat.

¹/₄ cup	all-purpose flour	60 mL
¹/₂ tsp.	each salt and pepper	2 mL
1 tsp.	dried basil or herbes de Provence	5 mL
1¹/₂ lbs.	pork loin chops, fat removed and cut into 1" (2.5 cm) pieces	750 g
1 cup	sliced carrots	250 mL
1 cup	sliced celery	250 mL
12 oz.	can light beer	341 mL
10 oz.	can golden mushroom soup	284 mL
1 tbsp.	cider or red wine vinegar	15 mL
1 tsp.	bottled minced garlic or 2 cloves crushed	5 mL
¹/₂ pkg.	fresh spinach	¹/₂ pkg.

- Preheat oven to 350°F (180°C).

- Combine flour, salt, pepper and herbs in a small plastic bag. Add pork cubes; toss and turn until coated. Shake off excess flour.

- In a 3-quart (3 L) covered ovenproof casserole, combine pork and remaining ingredients, except spinach. Cover and bake in the oven for 1¹/₂-2 hours, until meat is tender. Stir a couple of times.

- Use kitchen scissors to cut up spinach a little. Stir into casserole and return to the oven for 10 minutes.

Serves 6

GO WITHS – Oven-Baked Potatoes, page 82, Broccoli Salad, page 64, and crusty bread.

Slow-Cooker Method

Combine ingredients as for oven method; reserve spinach to cook on HIGH for about the last 10 minutes. Cook on HIGH for 3-4 hours or on LOW for 6-8 hours. Stir about 3 times, if you are at home.

Stove-Top Method

Prepare and combine ingredients in a Dutch oven or large cooking pot. Heat to boiling; reduce heat and cover. Simmer for 1-1¹/₂ hours. Stir 2-3 times. Add chopped spinach for last 5-10 minutes.

Cook's Tips

The spinach may be omitted, but it adds color, flavor and good nutrition.

The remainder of the spinach can be used in a salad, frittata, quiche or added to a curry dish, lasagne, soup or pasta . . . or use the whole package. Instead of chopping fresh spinach, hold a small bunch and snip spinach into the dish using clean kitchen scissors.

To thaw a frozen block of spinach for a recipe, put frozen spinach in a 1-quart (2 L) casserole in the microwave. Cover and microwave on HIGH for 3 minutes. Uncover. Cool slightly. Squeeze dry and chop.

STUDENT SURVIVAL OR BIG-BATCH COOKING

This chapter is for those whose time and energy is spent other than in their apartment and kitchen – time spent studying, working, traveling, etc. The recipes also work for single moms and dads who have the kids on weekends or 2 nights during the week, when larger amounts of food must be cooked and busy schedules kept.

It is also for those who like to cook in larger amounts and store it away, like an investment at the bank. They are single cooks and couples who feel that, "If I am going to cook and make a mess and spend all that time in the kitchen, I might as well make a bigger mess and make it worthwhile."

All the slow-cooker recipes give stove-top or oven methods as well.

SLOW-COOKING

Slow-cooking is quick-cooking. Just dump all the ingredients in the pot; put the lid on and go off and do something important, or not so important.

The bonus is good, nutritious food that fills your home or apartment with savory aromas.

The slow cooker can produce a meal for you, with more for another day, or it can produce a delicious, hearty meal for a gathering.

The most popular slow cooker is a continuous-heat model with a capacity of 4-6 quarts (4-6 L). The LOW heating coils are in the outer shell. The LOW setting is about 200°F (93°C) and the HIGH is at 300°F (150°C). Foods can cook on LOW for 6-10 hours and on HIGH for 2-4 hours. One hour on HIGH equals about 2 1/2 on LOW. So recipes taking 8-10 hours to cook on LOW can be cooked in half the time on HIGH. Temperatures do vary from cooker to cooker. A little trial and error will help you become familiar with yours and provide good food while you experiment.

You can buy a slow cooker for under $30.00. You may be lucky and inherit one from home or from an aunt, or find one at a garage sale walkabout. I like the original brand, "RIVAL".

For best results, read the manual or browse the slow cooker cookbooks in a library or bookstore.

There are a few practical points to remember about slow-cooking:

- Keep the lid on. Lifting the lid means heat loss.

- Check the food for doneness at the minimum cooking time suggested.

- Trim the fat from meat and poultry and remove poultry skin. If the finished dish has fat on the top, skim it off with a spoon.

- Taste during the last $1/2$ hour of cooking; add salt and pepper and additional herbs and spices, if needed. The long cooking time will have reduced the flavor of the original seasonings.

- For convenience and quick preparation, most of the recipes here do not brown the meat in advance of the cooking. Not browning the meat means some loss of the flavor and color. The addition of **herbs** and **seasonings**, and the use of **soy** and **Worcestershire** sauces help to color the sauces and make up for not browning. Canned **soups** add flavor, don't break down during the long cooking process and help to form a creamy flavorful sauce or gravy.

COOKING TIPS

- When adding frozen vegetables, thaw them in warm water first. Adding frozen vegetables cools the other ingredients.

- For quick assembly in the morning, before work or class, prepare the meat; cut all the vegetables and assemble the ingredients the night before. Store the vegetables in the fridge and add to the cooker in the morning.

- There are 2 reasons why we do not prepare the ingredients ahead and store them in the slow cooker in the fridge, then place the cooker in the heating unit. The ceramic liner will not cool down in the fridge to cool and protect the vegetables and meat, and the cold liner could crack when inserted in the heater unit.

- **Dense vegetables**, like **potatoes**, **carrots**, **turnips** and **parsnips**, take a long time to cook and are best cooked at the bottom of the casserole.

- **To maintain their color and texture**, add other vegetables like **peppers**, **zucchini**, **green beans**, **cabbage** and **dried fruit** in the last half hour or so. Some times, I precook them for 5 minutes in the microwave and add them and any juices to the ingredients in the slow cooker for the last 10 minutes of cooking time.

FOOD SAFETY AND SLOW COOKERS

Always cook and drain **ground meats** before adding them to the slow cooker. The reason is to kill any bacteria that may be present in the meat. Simply put the meat on to brown and cook while you are assembling the other ingredients that you need.

It is important to remove leftovers from the cooker as soon as you finish eating. Transfer leftovers to bowls; cover and refrigerate. **DO NOT store the ceramic bowl in the fridge with food in it** – the density of the bowl does not allow for quick cooling.

Bean and Vegetable Soup

This soup is easy to make and takes minutes to prepare. No fat, loaded with good nutrition and it's cheap, too! It is the guarantee of a quick meal at the end of a long busy day. **It also freezes well**.

6 cups	chicken OR vegetable broth	1.5 L
2 cups	dried bean soup mix, see tip below	500 mL
3-4	medium carrots, chopped	3-4
3	celery stalk, chopped	3
1	large onion, chopped	1
2 tbsp.	tomato paste OR ketchup	30 mL
1 tsp.	salt	5 mL
1/2 tsp.	pepper	2 mL
2 tsp.	Italian herb seasoning OR Cajun spice	10 mL
14 oz.	can diced tomatoes (any style)	398 mL

- Combine all ingredients, except tomatoes, in slow cooker. Cover and cook on LOW setting for 8-10 hours, or until the beans are tender. Rinse beans, discard any spoiled beans.

- Stir tomatoes in at the last. Increase heat to HIGH; cover and cook for 15-20 minutes to heat the tomatoes.

GO WITHS – Try one of the savory bread combos on page 21.

Stove-Top Method

Combine all ingredients, except tomatoes, in a large pot over medium-high heat. Bring to a boil and cook for 10 minutes. Skim off any foam that accumulates. Reduce heat and simmer for 1 1/2-2 hours, until beans are tender. Add tomatoes; increase heat a little and cook for about 10 minutes.

Cook's Tips

Buying the beans from the supermarket bulk bins or a bulk food store is the easiest. If you can't find the soup mix, buy 1 cup (250 mL) EACH of kidney beans and navy or white beans.

Second-day soups often require additional liquid. Add broth or tomato juice as needed.

Soup is a good place to use the water left over from cooking potatoes or other vegetables.

For added protein and flavor, add cooked ground meat to the slow cooker when you add the vegetables.

Here, too, is where you can use up any leftover bean salad or leftover portions of canned or cooked vegetables or tomatoes. Just add them to the soup near the beginning of the cooking time.

Add tomatoes to soups made with dried beans for just the last few minutes – it preserves their distinctive flavor and texture, which makes for a better soup. Also, the acid in the tomatoes impedes the cooking time of the beans.

Winter Vegetable Stew

Load the slow cooker in the morning – the good smells will welcome you home. Add rice and enjoy.

28 oz.	can tomatoes	796 mL
14 oz.	can vegetable broth, chicken OR beef broth	284 mL
1	medium carrot, coarsely chopped	1
1/2	green pepper, chopped	1/2
1	medium onion, chopped	1
2	celery stalks, diced	2
1 cup	coleslaw mix, chopped to finer pieces, OR chopped cabbage OR potato	250 mL
1/2 tsp.	dried italian herbs	2 mL
1/2 tsp.	dried basil leaves	2 mL
1 tsp.	salt	5 mL
1/4 tsp.	freshly ground pepper	1 mL
1 cup	uncooked instant rice OR small, shaped pasta	250 mL

- Combine all ingredients, except rice, in slow cooker. Cover and cook on LOW setting for 6-8 hours. The stew can cook a little longer if you will not be home until later.

- Add rice and cook for 15 minutes more.

Serves 3-4

GO WITHS – A **pita pocket** sprayed with oil, sprinkled with grated **cheese** and toasted in the toaster oven or under the broiler for a few minutes.

Stove-Top Method

Combine all ingredients, except rice, in a large pot over medium-high heat. Bring to a boil and cook for 5 minutes. Reduce heat and simmer for 30 minutes. Add rice and cook for about 5 minutes longer.

Variations

Add a can of drained **lentils** with the broth.

Add 1/2 lb. (250 g) browned **extra-lean ground beef**.

Cook's Tip

Make Vegetable Slaw, page 65, out of remaining cabbage or add chopped cabbage to any vegetable soup or stew.

Garden Vegetable Chili

After a summer visit to my sister's at the lake, my kids came home and said, "Why don't you put potatoes and carrots in chili like Auntie Jonine does?" So I did, and here it is.

1 lb.	extra-lean ground beef	500 g
1	large onion, chopped	1
2	celery stalks, cut in 1" (2.5 cm) pieces	2
2	carrots, cut in 1/2" (1.3 cm) slices	2
2	medium, thin-skinned potatoes, washed and cut into 1/2" (1.3 cm) pieces	2
28 oz.	can diced tomatoes or whole tomatoes, cut up	796 mL
10 oz.	can tomato sauce	284 mL
2-3 tbsp.	chili powder	30-45 mL
1-2 tsp.	ground cumin	5-10 mL
1/2 tsp.	cinnamon	2 mL
2x15.5 oz.	cans kidney beans, rinsed and drained	2x425 mL

- Heat a large non-stick skillet over medium-high heat. Add meat and cook until no pink remains. Use paper towels to absorb the fat from the beef.

- Combine all ingredients, except beans, in a slow cooker.

- Cook on MEDIUM-HIGH until beef is lightly browned. Break up with a spoon as it cooks.

- Cover and cook on LOW for 8-10 hours.

- Add drained beans for the last 15-30 minutes of cooking time.

- Increase heat to HIGH to cook the beans a little faster.

Serves 3-4

Stove-Top Method

Combine all ingredients, except beans, in a large pot over medium-high heat. Bring to a boil; reduce heat and cook for about 20 minutes, until vegetables are partially cooked. Add beans and cook for another 20-30 minutes.

Variations

VEGETARIAN CHILI – Omit the meat. Assemble all of the other ingredients and add to the slow cooker. Cook as directed.

Substitute 1 can **EACH** of **black beans** and **chickpeas** for the kidney beans or use 1 can EACH of **kidney beans** and either **black beans or chickpeas**.

Try the **Veggie Chili** 1, 2, 3, page 79. It's quick and easy.

Cook's Tip

If your chili is too hot (spicy), add 1/2 tsp. (2 mL) of sugar to 1 quart (1 L) of chili to lower the heat level.

Cajun-Style Steak

This lightly spiced steak is saucy, like a stew. Round steak is lean and relatively inexpensive. It is not necessary to brown the meat but browning the meat and sautéing the vegetables adds wonderful flavors to the sauce. The amount and choice of vegetables are yours. This recipe is loaded with good flavor as well as protein and iron.

3 tbsp.	flour	45 mL
	sprinkle of salt and pepper	
1 lb.	round steak, cut into 8 pieces	500 g
1 tbsp.	vegetable oil	15 mL
1	onion chopped	1
2	celery stalks, sliced	2
2	carrots, sliced	2
1/4 tsp.	cayenne pepper OR hot pepper sauce	1 mL
14 oz.	can chili-style stewed or diced tomatoes	398 mL
1/2	EACH green pepper and red pepper, chopped (optional)	1/2

- Place flour, salt and pepper in a small bowl or plastic bag; add beef and toss to coat, pressing flour into meat.

- Heat a large non-stick skillet over medium-high heat. Add oil; add meat and cook until browned on both sides. Remove to a plate. Add onion, celery and carrots to pan. Cook and stir until onions are softened. Add cayenne.

- Place browned meat and accumulated juices in slow cooker; add sautéed vegetables. Rinse out the pan with a little of the juice from the tomatoes or water. Stir, scraping up the brown bits. Pour juice, brown bits and tomatoes into the cooker.

- Stir a little; cover and cook for 6-8 hours on LOW. Add peppers; cover and cook on HIGH for 15 minutes.

Serves 3-4

GO WITHS – Mashed potatoes and garlic bread.

Stove-Top Method

Returned browned meat and juices to skillet with vegetables. Bring to a boil; reduce heat; cover and cook for about 30 minutes, until meat and vegetables are tender.

Variations

Add any vegetables that you like or that you have. Also, try **parsnip**, **potato**, **cabbage** and **turnip**.

Cook's Tips

For a milder flavor, omit **cayenne pepper** and use diced **tomatoes**, original style or garlic and herb tomatoes. No chili-style tomatoes? Add diced tomatoes and 2 tsp. (10 mL) **chili powder** and 1/2 tsp. (2 mL) **cumin**.

Chuckwagon Soupy Stew

With or without meat, this quickly combined meal is loaded with goodness.

1 lb.	stewing beef, cubed (more or less is OK too)	500 g
1 cup	EACH sliced celery and carrots	250 mL
2	garlic cloves, crushed (optional)	2
10 oz.	EACH can beef bouillon and water OR vegetable broth	284 mL
14 oz.	can diced or stewed tomatoes	398 mL
1/2 cup	barley, rinsed	125 mL
14 oz.	can beans in tomato sauce	398 mL
1 pkg.	dried onion soup mix	1 pkg.
1/2 tsp.	dried thyme	2 mL
	salt and pepper to taste (There is salt in the soup mix! Taste first.)	

- Place all ingredients in a slow cooker. Stir to combine. Cook for 4 hours on HIGH or 8-10 hours on LOW heat.

Serves 3-4

GO WITHS – Whole-grain bread, plus an apple for dessert.

Stove-Top Method

- Combine all ingredients in a pasta pot or Dutch oven. Bring to a boil and cook for 10 minutes, stirring a few times. Reduce heat to simmer; cover and cook for 2-3 hours, until the meat is tender.

- For a no-meat version, cook until the barley is tender, about 1 hour.

Variations

VEGETARIAN STEW – Substitute a second can of **beans in tomato sauce** for the beef chunks. More vegetables? Try sliced zucchini or chopped cabbage.

GO WITHS – A green salad and a fruit dessert . . . cookies, too!

If you have time, to make this good stew absolutely delicious, brown the meat in a little vegetable oil. Remove beef to a plate. Add a little more oil to the pan and sauté the celery and carrots, then dump it all in the slow cooker. Proceed as above.

Beef Stew

Use a slow cooker or an oven. Share this easy-to-make stew with a friend and bank 1-2 meals for the freezer. There is no need to brown the meat, just put everything in the pot.

2 tbsp.	all-purpose flour	30 mL
1/4 tsp.	EACH freshly ground black pepper and salt	1 mL
3/4-1 lb.	round steak, all fat removed, cut into bite-sized pieces	350-500 g
10 oz.	can low-sodium beef broth OR beer	284 mL
1	potato, cut into bite-sized pieces	1
1 cup	baby carrots, cut in half	250 mL
1	small onion, chopped	1
1 tsp.	beef bouillon granules	5 mL
1/2 tsp.	Mrs. Dash original OR dried thyme	2 mL
1 tsp.	Worcestershire sauce	5 mL
2 tbsp.	tomato paste OR ketchup	30 mL

- Preheat oven to 325°F (160°C).
- Combine flour, pepper and salt in a plastic bag. Add meat. Hold the top of the bag to seal, and shake until the meat is well coated.
- Remove meat from bag, shake off excess flour and place in a Dutch oven or other ovenproof lidded dish. Add remaining ingredients. Stir so that ingredients are evenly mixed. Cover; place in oven and cook for 2-3 hours, stirring once or twice.

Serves 4

Slow-Cooker Method

Prepare meat and vegetables as above. Add to a 3 1/2-4 quart (3.5-4 L) slow cooker. Cook on HIGH for 4-5 hours, or on LOW for 9-10 hours, or until meat is tender.

Gremolata

This is a perfect accent to Pork and Chicken Tagine, pages 130, 149, and curry dishes. I like the burst of flavor that it brings to a steak as well.

2	garlic cloves, minced	2
1/4 cup	finely chopped parsley	60 mL
1 tbsp.	finely grated lemon zest	15 mL
	olive oil to moisten, about 1 tsp. (5 mL)	

- Combine all ingredients in a small bowl. Drop 1-2 spoonfuls onto the top of the Tagine or the curry dish, or the Gremolata can be placed on the table in a small dish as a condiment.

Cook's Tips

Stews, sauces and most soups taste much better on the second day, when the savory mixtures of spices and herbs have a chance to blend and mellow.

Barley, pasta, rice and beans continue to absorb the liquid in soups and stews. When reheating, if you need to thin down the soups and stews, just add more of the broth or other liquid in the recipe.

DESSERTS &
SWEET TREATS

Here are pared-down cake, cookie and dessert ideas and recipes. They are quick to make and, as desserts go, they are healthy. They contain fruits, nuts and cereals – even the chocolate cake is lower fat and has rolled oats in it.

The sugary, chocolaty treats and snacks are comfort food and just plain good to eat. Enjoy . . . in moderation.

My daughter-in-law Jennifer Ryan is a great cook. Her help and input is very evident in the creation of these wonderful desserts and treats.

To make sure that dessert adds to your daily nutritional needs, and not to your waistline, choose one of these simple, satisfying and quick-to-prepare treats.

- A perfect apple, orange or pear.

- Fresh blueberries, strawberries, raspberries, grapes or sliced peaches in a bowl with a spoonful of sour cream or plain yogurt mixed with a little brown sugar.

- Top fresh berries, sliced peaches, nectarines or mangos with whipped cream flavored with vanilla or a splash of orange liqueur. Sprinkle with finely chopped chocolate or crystallized ginger for an elegant effect.

- Top orange and banana slices with flavored or plain yogurt.

- Single-serving cans of peaches, pears, pineapple or applesauce, try pineapple or peaches with cottage cheese and cinnamon-sprinkled applesauce.

- **BROWNIE SUNDAE** – Top a bakery **brownie** with a scoop of **ice cream**; add **toasted pecans or almonds, chocolate sauce**.

- **COOKIE PARFAIT** – Layer **ice cream**, broken **cookie pieces**, ice cream and more cookie pieces. Add fruit if you have it, and **chocolate sauce**.

- **Angel food cake** with fresh or thawed **strawberries** and **chocolate sauce** OR angel food cake with **strawberries or apricots** marinated in **Grand Marnier. Ice cream**, too!

Cook's Tips

Use **icing (confectioner's) sugar** to sweeten **whipped cream** – it gives a smoother texture and it stabilizes the cream. Before beating, be sure to chill bowl and beaters for 20 minutes.

LOW-FAT WHIPPED TOPPING – Slightly frozen (with ice crystals) **evaporated milk** can be whipped and used as a low-fat, less-expensive whipped cream substitute. Add 1 tbsp. (15 mL) **lemon juice** to 1/2 cup (125 mL) **milk** and whip until stiff. Volume should triple. Add **sugar** to taste.

FRUIT SALADS

Make fruit salad when you find you have too much fruit on hand. It keeps well in the fridge and it is very adaptable. Top cereal with fruit salad or top fruit salad with flavored yogurt or ice cream. Dress it up with a little liqueur and make a parfait or an instant trifle.

Here are a few things that make a better fruit salad:

- Cut hard fruits, like apples and pineapples, in ¼-½" (6.3 mm-1.3 cm) pieces.

- Add **bananas** and **blueberries** shortly before serving – **bananas** look very tired and mushy the next day and **blueberries** color the juice.

- If you need more fruit, or a starter for a company salad, add a small **can of pineapple** tidbits or some fruit from a bag of **frozen mixed fruit**.

- Stirring in ¼-½ cup (60-125 mL) **orange juice** adds flavor and the juice prevents the fruit from turning brown. A squeeze of **lemon or lime juice** is good too.

Fruit Salad Topping Ideas
vanilla yogurt
sour cream, sugar, toasted almond or pecans
yogurt mixed with a little honey and orange or lime juice concentrates
vanilla ice cream
lime or lemon sherbet or sorbet
sour cream and toasted coconut

SUNDAES AND PARFAITS

Don't overlook ice cream when you're waiting for dessert inspiration to strike. It's quick and easy – and loved by kids and adults alike. When you want to fuss a little, try these dress-up ideas.

Sundaes

Sundaes can be as simple or elaborate as you like:

- CLASSIC HOT FUDGE SUNDAE – Pour warmed **chocolate sauce** over a scoop of **vanilla ice cream**. Add **toasted pecans or almonds**.

- **Vanilla ice cream**, pure **maple syrup**, and **toasted pecans** are an elegant combination.

A fun idea for entertaining is a Sundae Bar:

Arrange **ice cream** (1 or 2 flavors), a scoop, dishes and spoons at the end of a table or counter, and set out dishes of as many toppings as you like. Let your guests create their own masterpieces.

Sundae Topping Ideas
chocolate and/or strawberry sauces
chocolate and/or caramel sauces
Skor® toffee bits
mini marshmallows
fresh berries
chopped fresh fruit

shredded coconut
Smarties or M&Ms
chopped oreo cookies
brownie chunks or slices
toasted nuts – walnuts, pecans, peanuts
and almonds

Parfaits

Layer individual parfaits in small glass serving bowls or stemmed dessert dishes. Alternate **ice cream** with broken **cookie chunks or brownie pieces** (homemade, from a mix, or purchased from a bakery), and top with **chocolate or strawberry sauce** and toasted **nuts**.

Chocolate Sauce

This can be stored in a jar in the fridge for up to 2 weeks. It gets quite thick when refrigerated, so warm in the microwave for 30 seconds or so to make it pourable. This sauce can also be used to make the world's richest hot chocolate – just stir 1-2 large spoonfuls into a cup of hot milk.

1 tbsp.	butter OR margarine	15 mL
2 tbsp.	cocoa	30 mL
2 tsp.	instant coffee powder	10 mL
1/3 cup	white OR brown sugar	75 mL
1/4 cup	corn syrup	60 mL
1/4 cup	milk	60 mL
1/2 tsp.	vanilla	2 mL
pinch	cinnamon	pinch

- Combine all ingredients, except vanilla and cinnamon, in a small saucepan. Heat over medium heat until boiling. Let it boil, stirring constantly, for 2 minutes.
- Remove from heat and stir in vanilla and cinnamon.

Makes about 3/4 cup (175 mL)

Variations

MEXICAN CHOCOLATE SAUCE – Increase **cinnamon** to 1/3 tsp. (1.5 mL).

RUM OR GRAND MARNIER CHOCOLATE SAUCE – Omit cinnamon and vanilla and add 1-2 tsp. (5-10 mL) **rum or Grand Marnier**. (Try the miniature bottles.)

GINGER CHOCOLATE SAUCE – Omit cinnamon and add 3-4 tsp. (15-20 mL) finely chopped **crystallized ginger** with the vanilla.

MINT OR ALMOND CHOCOLATE SAUCE – Omit cinnamon and vanilla and add 2-3 drops of **peppermint or almond extract**. Taste and add 1-2 drops more if needed.

Nutrition Note

A Cornell University study shows that **hot cocoa** contains more antioxidents per serving than red wine (almost double) or green or black teas (triple). Use 2 tbsp. (30 mL) **cocoa powder** with 1 cup (250 mL) **skim milk** and an **artificial sweetener**.

Strawberry Sauce

A quick and delicious topper for ice cream, cake, pancakes or waffles.

2 cups	strawberries, fresh or frozen (unsweetened, loose pack)	500 mL
1/4 cup	orange juice	60 mL
3 tbsp.	honey OR sugar	45 mL
1 tsp.	lemon juice	5 mL
1/4 cup	water	60 mL
2 tsp.	cornstarch	10 mL

- If using fresh strawberries, rinse and hull. Coarsely chop or slice fresh or frozen berries.

- Mix berries, orange juice and honey in a small saucepan. Stir over medium-high heat until ingredients are combined and juices are bubbling.

- Whisk together water and cornstarch. Stir into hot sauce. Return sauce to a boil. Stir and cook until mixture has thickened, about 2 minutes.

- Remove from heat and stir in lemon juice. Cool sauce and serve, or store, covered, in the fridge.

Makes about 2 cups (500 mL)

Variations

Two-Fruit Sauce – Replace 1 cup (250 mL) of **strawberries** with **blueberries or** chopped **peaches**. If you prefer a sweeter sauce, increase the sugar or honey. For a grown-up version, stir 1-2 tbsp. (15-30 mL) **Grand Marnier or Triple Sec** into cooled sauce.

Brown Sugar and Rum-Baked Bananas

Mellow and rich – a luscious dessert.

1-2	ripe bananas, peeled and halved lengthwise	1-2
2-4 tsp.	brown sugar	10-20 mL
1-2 tsp.	soft butter	5-10 mL
2-4 tsp.	dark rum	10-20 mL
1/2-1 cup	vanilla OR chocolate ice cream	125-250 mL

- Preheat oven to 400°F (200°C).

- Place banana halves in a small baking dish. Sprinkle with brown sugar and dot with butter. Spoon rum over bananas.

- Bake until sugar topping is bubbling and caramelized, about 8-10 minutes.

- Serve hot caramelized bananas with ice cream.

Serves 1 or 2

Pictured on page 171

Banana Fool

Mash a ripe **banana** with a fork (easiest to do on a side plate). Add about $1/4$ cup (60 mL) plain, vanilla or tropical fruit-flavored **yogurt or whipped cream**. Mix well and pour into a small glass serving dish. Chill in the freezer for about 15 minutes before serving.

Variations

BERRY OR PEACH FOOL – Try 1 cup (250 mL) mashed **strawberries**, **raspberries or peaches** mixed with the yogurt and chilled. My granddaughter Elena's favorite is **wild blueberries** and **yogurt** topped with broken **cookie** pieces.

Peach and Berries Brulée

This is sooo good. It looks very elegant and will impress everyone – or make it just for you – it's that easy!

1-2 cups	fresh strawberries OR raspberries OR frozen mixed fruit, the kind with peach slices and mixed berries	250-500 mL
1 cup	vanilla yogurt OR sour cream OR whipped cream brown sugar for topping	250 mL

- Place fresh or frozen fruit in a shallow ovenproof dish, to hold the fruit in a single or double layer.

- Spread yogurt, sour cream or whipped cream over fruit, covering fruit completely and sealing to all edges.

- Refrigerate for 1-2 hours, until using.

- Sprinkle brown sugar over topping in a thin even layer. Place baking dish on a cookie sheet or pan.

- Preheat broiler and broil until brown sugar bubbles and caramelizes, 2-3 minutes. Watch carefully so it doesn't burn.

- You can serve it now or refrigerate for 1-2 hours.

Variation

Freshly made or canned **applesauce**, sprinkled with a little **cinnamon**, may be substituted for the fresh or frozen fruit.

Cook's Tip

If using plain yogurt, sweeten with a little sugar.

Fresh Strawberry Pie

Beautiful to look at, delicious to eat, easy to prepare. Fresh strawberries in a nutty chocolate cookie crust – the ultimate celebration of strawberry season. The pie comes together quickly, but must be made early in the day to leave time for chilling.

Nutty Chocolate Crust

1 1/2 cups	chocolate wafer crumbs	375 mL
1/4 cup	finely chopped almonds OR pecans	60 mL
1/4 cup	butter, melted	60 mL

Strawberry Filling

2 lbs.	strawberries (approx. 6 cups), washed and hulled	1 kg
1 cup	sugar	250 mL
3 tbsp.	cornstarch	45 mL
1/4 cup	water	60 mL
pinch	salt	pinch
1 tsp.	finely grated lemon zest	5 mL
	whipped cream, vanilla ice cream OR vanilla yogurt for garnish	

- Preheat oven to 350°F (180°C).

- Stir crust ingredients together in a medium bowl until well combined. Use your fingers to pat the mixture onto the bottom and sides of an ungreased 9" (23 cm) pie pan. Bake for 8 minutes. Cool completely.

- Use a potato masher or fork in a small bowl to mash enough strawberries to equal 1 cup (250 mL) .

- In a heavy-bottomed pot, combine mashed strawberries and sugar. Heat over medium heat just until boiling.

- Meanwhile, whisk cornstarch and water together. Whisk cornstarch mixture into boiling strawberry mixture and continue to cook, stirring occasionally, until mixture thickens, about 5 minutes. Remove from heat and add salt and lemon zest. Let cool for 10 minutes.

- Fill crust with remaining strawberries (cut any large ones in half, leave the small ones whole). Pour cooked mixture evenly over strawberries. Refrigerate at least 3 hours before cutting into wedges.

- Serve garnished with whipped cream, ice cream or yogurt.

Serves 8-10

MAKE-AHEAD – Prepare crust and store at room temperature for up to 2 days.

SUPER-QUICK – Use a prepared **graham wafer or chocolate cookie crust**.

Variations

This method can be used to make a variety of fresh fruit pies. Try using different cookie crumbs for the crust – **gingersnaps** and **shortbread cookies** are both good. **Peaches or blueberries** can be substituted for the strawberries.

Oatmeal Chocolate Chip Cookies

Perfect with a cold glass of milk. Use butter or margarine if you like your cookies chewy, shortening if you like them crisp. Use ¹/₄ cup (60 mL) of each if you want the best of both worlds.

¹/₂ cup	butter, margarine OR shortening, at room temperature	125 mL
¹/₂ cup	brown sugar, firmly packed	125 mL
¹/₃ cup	white sugar	75 mL
1 tbsp.	water	15 mL
1	egg	1
¹/₂ tsp.	vanilla (optional)	2 mL
³/₄ cup	all-purpose flour	175 mL
¹/₄ tsp.	baking soda	1 mL
¹/₄ tsp.	salt	1 mL
1¹/₄ cups	quick-cooking oats (not instant)	300 mL
¹/₂ cup	chocolate chips	125 mL
¹/₂ cup	coconut or coarsely chopped nuts (optional)	125 mL

- Preheat oven to 375°F (190°C).

- In a medium bowl, use an electric mixer to beat butter until creamy. Add sugars and continue beating until mixture is light and fluffy. Add water and egg and beat well.

- Combine flour, soda and salt in a small bowl. Add flour mixture to butter mixture and beat until just combined.

- Add oats, chocolate chips and nuts, if using, and mix well.

- Drop dough by rounded spoonfuls onto an ungreased cookie sheet.

- Bake on the middle oven rack until edges are lightly browned, about 10-12 minutes. If you like your cookies crispy, bake 1-2 minutes longer.

- Cool 1 minute on cookie sheet, then remove to a wire rack to cool completely.

Makes 24 cookies

Variations

OATMEAL RAISIN COOKIES – Follow method above. Substitute ¹/₂ cup **raisins** (125 mL) for chocolate chips, and stir ¹/₂ tsp. (2 mL) **cinnamon** into the flour mixture.

OATMEAL TOFFEE COOKIES – Stir ¹/₂ cup (125 mL) **Skor® toffee bits** into either the chocolate chip OR raisin version.

FOLK FESTIVAL COOKIES – Stir ¹/₄ cup (60 mL) coarsely ground **flaxseed** and ¹/₄ cup (60 mL) toasted **raw sunflower seeds** into either the chocolate chip OR raisin version.

Pictured on page 171

Cook's Tip

Double the recipe for more cookies!

Triple Chocolate Cookies

These cookies pack an intense chocolate hit – a cold glass of milk is a mandatory accompaniment! The coffee powder heightens the chocolate flavor, but feel free to omit it if you don't have any on hand.

1/2 cup	butter OR margarine	125 mL
1/2 cup	brown sugar, packed	125 mL
1/3 cup	white sugar	75 mL
2 tsp.	instant coffee powder	10 mL
1 tbsp.	warm water	15 mL
1	egg	1
1 1/4 cups	flour	300 mL
1/3 cup	unsweetened cocoa powder	75 mL
1/2 tsp.	baking soda	2 mL
1/4 tsp.	salt	1 mL
1/2 tsp.	cinnamon	2 mL
1/2 cup	chocolate chips	125 mL
1/2 cup	white chocolate chips	125 mL
1/2 cup	chopped nuts (optional)	125 mL

- Preheat oven to 375°F (190°C).

- Use an electric mixer to cream butter and sugars together in a large bowl. Dissolve coffee powder in water and add to bowl. Add egg and beat well.

- In a small bowl, combine flour, cocoa, baking soda, salt and cinnamon. Add to creamed mixture and beat until just combined.

- Stir in chocolate chips and nuts, if using.

- Shape dough into 1" (2.5 cm) balls. Place on ungreased baking sheets and flatten slightly.

- Bake on the middle oven rack for 12-15 minutes. Let cool on pan for 2-3 minutes before removing to a rack to cool completely.

Makes 24 cookies

Pictured on page 171

Cook's Tips

Double the recipe for more cookies! You will want to share with a friend.

These are the cookies that make the elegant Sundaes and Parfaits on pages 161 and 162.

Nutty Chocolate Toffee Crunch

Easy and addictive.

9	graham wafers (approx.)	9
1/3 cup	butter	75 mL
1/3 cup	brown sugar	75 mL
1/3 cup	coarsely chopped nuts – walnuts, pecans, almonds OR cashews are all good	75 mL
1/3 cup	chocolate chips	75 mL

- Preheat oven to 325°F (160°C).

- Line an 8" (20 cm) square pan with graham wafers, breaking to fit where necessary.

- Melt butter in a small saucepan over medium heat. Stir in brown sugar and bring to a boil. Reduce heat and boil for 1 minute, stirring constantly. Remove from heat and immediately pour over graham wafers. Use a knife or rubber spatula to quickly spread the toffee to completely and evenly cover the graham wafers. Sprinkle with nuts.

- Bake for about 10 minutes, until browned and bubbly. Immediately sprinkle with chocolate chips. Let cool slightly before using a sharp knife to cut into 2" (5 cm) squares.

Makes 16 squares

Nutrition Note

Nuts are not only delicious – they are good for you.

Daily consumption of about **1 handful (1/4 cup/60 mL) shelled nuts or 2 handfuls of nuts in the shell** provides maximum benefits, according to several recent studies, which have shown that people who regularly consume nuts have fewer heart attacks and strokes, lower blood pressure, less risk of developing type 2 diabetes and dementia. **The nurses' study also indicated that this level of nut consumption did not result in weight gains.**

Almonds, walnuts, hazelnuts, pecans, peanuts, pistachios, macadamia nuts and **cashews,** all help to lower cholesterol levels. Nuts are high in protein and fiber, and are good sources of vitamin E, folic acid and many minerals. While nuts are high in fat, nut fats are polyunsaturated and monounsaturated.

For the best health benefits, add a variety of raw or roasted nuts to stir-fries, salads, stews, desserts, or just enjoy them as a satisfying snack.

Peanut Butter Granola Bars

Most granola bars are laden with oil and sugar. This not-too-sweet version features honey and protein-packed peanut butter. They make a great recess or coffee-break snack, and are easy enough for kids to make, with a little adult help.

1/4 cup	honey	60 mL
1/4 cup	peanut butter	60 mL
1/2 tsp.	vanilla	2 mL
1 1/4 cups	quick-cooking oats (not instant)	300 mL
1/2 cup	raisins	125 mL
2 tbsp.	chopped nuts, coconut or sunflower seeds	30 mL
2 tbsp.	sesame seeds	30 mL

- Preheat oven to 350°F (180°C).

- Combine honey, peanut butter and vanilla in a small microwaveable bowl or measuring cup. Microwave on HIGH for 45 seconds, or until melted. Stir thoroughly.

- Combine dry ingredients in a large bowl. Pour peanut butter mixture over and mix thoroughly. Pat into an ungreased 8" (20 cm) square pan and bake for 15-20 minutes, just until golden. Cool completely before slicing into bars.

Makes 16 bars

Variations

These bars are infinitely variable. Increase nutrition by stirring in 2 tbsp. (30 mL) **powdered milk**, 2 tbsp. (30 mL) coarsely ground **flaxseed**, and/or 2 tbsp. (30 mL) **wheat germ**. Any **dried fruit** (chopped dried **apricots**, dried **cranberries or dates**) may be substituted for the raisins – or omit the raisins and use **chocolate chips** instead.

These bars are also great crumbled and sprinkled over ice cream, yogurt, breakfast cereal or fruit salad.

Cook's Tip

Products like whole-wheat flour, bran, wheat germ, pine nuts and walnuts do not have a long shelf life. It is best to buy them in small quantities and store them in the fridge or a cool place.

Apple Crisp

So good! Try it with peaches too. Leftovers can be part of breakfast.

2	small apples, peeled and sliced	2
	a sprinkle of sugar, salt and cinnamon	
2 tbsp.	all-purpose flour OR whole-wheat flour	30 mL
2 tbsp.	brown sugar	30 mL
1 tbsp.	quick-cooking oats OR wheat germ	15 mL
2 tbsp.	cold butter OR margarine	30 mL

- Place apple slices in small bowl. Sprinkle with sugar, salt and cinnamon.

- Combine flour, sugar and oats. Use your fingers to rub butter into dry ingredients; continue until the mixture appears crumbly.

- Sprinkle flour mixture on top of apples and bake at 375°F (190°C) for 30-35 minutes, until topping is lightly browned.

- Serve as is or with cream or vanilla yogurt.

Makes 1 large serving

For **6** servings – Use 8 apples and an 8 or 9" (20 or 23 cm) square baking dish. Sprinkle apples with 3 tsp. (15 mL) **sugar** and a little **salt** and **cinnamon**.

Topping for **6** servings – In a bowl, combine 1 cup (250 mL) EACH **all-purpose flour and brown sugar**. Add ½ cup (125 mL) cold **butter** cut into small pieces. Use a pastry, blender, or 2 table knives, scissor style, to "cut" the butter into the flour mixture. The butter should be in pea-sized pieces. Scatter the topping over the fruit. Bake at 375°F (190°C) until the topping is brown and the fruit bubbly, about 50 minutes. Serve with cream or ice cream.

Variations

Apple Crisp with Dried Cranberries and Blueberries – Add a few **raisins or dried cranberries and/or blueberries** to the apples and add 1 tbsp. (15 mL) chopped **pecans** to the crumb mixture.

Pictured opposite

Peaches and blueberries or rhubarb and strawberries are also good fruit combinations to replace apples. Rhubarb will require another spoonful of sugar.

Cook's Tip

Time Saver – Slice apples into microwaveable bowl, sprinkle with salt and cinnamon. Cover with waxed paper. Microwave on HIGH for 2 minutes. While apples are cooking, prepare topping. Sprinkle topping on heated apples and bake at 375°F (190°C) for 20 minutes, or until the apples are bubbly and topping is browned.

DESERTS

Lemon Squares

These are easy to make, sweet, tangy and totally addictive.

1 cup	unbleached all-purpose flour	250 mL
1/2 cup	butter	125 mL
1/4 cup	packed brown sugar	60 mL

Lemon Filling

1 cup	white sugar	250 mL
1 tsp.	grated lemon rind	5 mL
3 tbsp.	lemon juice (juice of 1 lemon)	45 mL
2 tbsp.	unbleached all-purpose flour	30 mL
1/2 tsp.	baking powder	2 mL
2	eggs, lightly beaten	2

- Preheat oven to 350°F (180°C). Grease a 9" (23 cm) square baking pan.

- **For the base**, mix the first 3 ingredients in a small bowl. Use your fingers to blend until crumbly. Press crumbs into the bottom of the pan and bake for about 15 minutes, or until lightly browned at the edges.

- **For the filling**, while the base cooks, combine remaining ingredients in a bowl. Pour over the cooked base.

- Bake for 25-30 minutes, or until lightly browned at the edges and barely set in the middle.

- Let cool completely. Use a sharp knife to cut into small squares.

Makes 36 squares

STORAGE – These store well in a tightly closed container. They freeze well too.

Variations

For a special presentation, cover with a light sifting of icing sugar and place in small, colored, paper baking cups.

Oh Henry Bars

A quick energy boost with peanut butter and chocolate flavors.

²/₃ cup	butter	150 mL
1 cup	brown sugar	250 mL
4 cups	quick-cooking rolled oats	1 L
¹/₂ cup	corn syrup	125 mL
1 tsp.	vanilla	5 mL
pinch	salt	pinch
1 cup	semisweet chocolate chips	250 mL
1 cup	peanut butter	250 mL
1¹/₂ cups	coarsely chopped unsalted peanuts	375 mL

- Preheat oven to 350°F (180°C). Grease a 9 x 13″ (23 x 33 cm) pan.

- In a large bowl, cream butter and sugar. Add rolled oats, syrup, salt and vanilla. Press firmly into a pan.

- Bake for 15 minutes. Cool slightly.

- Melt chocolate chips and peanut butter in a double boiler or microwave. Pour over base. Sprinkle with chopped peanuts, pressing nuts gently into base. Refrigerate until set. Cut into bars.

Makes 18-21 large bars

Sweet Marie Squares

No-bake treats.

3 cups	Rice Krispies	750 mL
1 cup	chopped peanuts (optional)	250 mL
1 cup	peanut butter	250 mL
1 cup	chocolate chips	250 mL
¹/₂ cup	corn syrup	125 mL
¹/₂ cup	brown sugar	125 mL
1 tsp.	vanilla	5 mL

- Grease an 8″ (20 cm) square pan.

- In a large bowl, combine Rice Krispies and nuts, if using.

- In a large saucepan over medium heat, melt peanut butter and chocolate chips with corn syrup and sugar.

- Stir to blend (do NOT boil). Add vanilla. Pour over Rice Krispies and nuts. Press into pan. Refrigerate until set. Cut into squares.

Makes 16-25 squares

Snacking Cake

Easy, easy, easy, and it even tastes great. Dress it up with a little frosting, page 176 or 177, and it is a birthday cake.

¹/₂ pkg.	spice cake mix (just over2 cups/500 mL)	¹/₂ pkg.
1	egg	1
¹/₄ cup	vegetable oil	60 mL
¹/₂ cup	fine or medium sweetened, shredded or flaked coconut	125 mL
¹/₂ cup	water OR milk	125 mL
	white sugar for sprinkling	

- Preheat oven to 375°F (180°C). Grease an 8" (20 cm) square baking pan.

- Combine all ingredients in a medium bowl. Blend well. Spread batter in pan. Bake for 25-30 minutes, until cake is lightly browned and set in the center.

- Sprinkle cake with sugar. Cool completely and cut into squares.

Makes 16 squares

Chocolate Cake

Moist and delicious. Serve with ice cream and thawed frozen raspberries for a super dessert.

¹/₂ cup	quick-cooking rolled oats	125 mL
1 cup	boiling water OR coffee	250 mL
¹/₄ cup	vegetable oil	60 mL
¹/₄ cup	cocoa powder	60 mL
1 tsp.	EACH salt and vanilla	5 mL
1 cup	unbleached, all-purpose flour	250 mL
1 cup	brown sugar	250 mL
1 tsp.	EACH baking soda and baking powder	5 mL
2	eggs	2

- Preheat oven to 350°F (180°C). Grease an 8" (20 cm) square pan.

- In a small bowl, combine oats and water. Let cool.

- Meanwhile, in a small bowl, combine remaining ingredients. Stir in oat mixture, spread in pan and bake for 35 minutes.

- Cool and frost with Chocolate Butter Icing, page 176, or sprinkle with icing (confectioner's) sugar.

Makes 16 squares

Applesauce Spice Cake

This is an old-fashioned spice cake. It's great served plain, topped with whipped cream, or iced with butter icing, see below. For a new taste top the cake with Orange Butter Icing, see page 177, and chopped walnuts or pecans.

1/3 cup	vegetable oil	75 mL
2/3 cup	brown sugar	150 mL
1	egg	1
1 cup	all-purpose flour	250 mL
1 tsp.	baking powder	5 mL
1/4 tsp.	salt	1 mL
1 tbsp.	cinnamon	15 mL
1/2 tsp.	nutmeg	2 mL
2/3 cup	unsweetened applesauce	150 mL
1/2 cup	raisins	125 mL
1/2 cup	chopped walnuts OR pecans	125 mL

- Preheat oven to 350°F (180°C). Lightly grease an 8″ (20 cm) square cake pan.

- In a large bowl, combine oil, sugar, and egg.

- In a small bowl, combine flour, baking powder, salt, cinnamon and nutmeg.

- Add about 1/2 the flour mixture to the oil mixture. Mix gently but thoroughly. Add the applesauce and mix thoroughly. Add remaining flour mixture and mix gently, **just until combined**. Gently stir in raisins and nuts.

- Pour batter into prepared pan. Bake for 30-35 minutes, or until cake begins to pull away from the sides of the pan and a toothpick inserted in the center of the cake comes out clean.

- Ice with Butter Icing, if you wish.

Makes 16 squares

BUTTER ICING/FROSTING – In a small bowl, using an electric mixer, beat 2 tbsp. (30 mL) **soft butter or margarine**, 1 cup (250 mL) **icing (confectioner's) sugar**, 1 tsp. (2 mL) **vanilla** and enough **milk or cream** to make a creamy spreadable icing, about 1-2 tbsp. (15-30 mL).

CHOCOLATE BUTTER ICING/FROSTING – **Omit vanilla** and add 2 tbsp. (30 mL) **cocoa** to Butter Icing.

Cook's Tips

If you wish to remove the cake from the pan, add a piece of waxed or parchment paper to the pan bottom before baking the cake.

Cake can be covered with plastic wrap or aluminum foil and stored in the fridge for several days.

Banana Cake

When you have 2 tired looking bananas, very ripe and very sweet, make a banana cake. You may ice this cake, but it is not necessary; for a quick dress up, sprinkle with sugar or a little sifted icing sugar.

1/2 cup	butter OR solid margarine at room temperature	125 mL
1 cup	white sugar	250 mL
1	large egg	1
1 tsp.	vanilla	5 mL
2 cups	unbleached all-purpose flour	500 mL
1 tsp.	baking soda	5 mL
pinch	salt	pinch
3/4 cup	mashed bananas	175 mL
1/2 cup	low-fat sour cream OR yogurt	125 mL

- Line an 8" (20 cm) square pan with waxed paper. (Cut a square of waxed paper the same size as the pan and place on the bottom of the pan.)

- Heat oven to 350°F (180°C).

- In a large bowl, using an electric mixer, beat butter until smooth; gradually add sugar and beat until well combined, 3-5 minutes. Add egg and vanilla and beat until smooth and fluffy looking, about 2 minutes.

- Combine flour, baking soda and salt in a small bowl. Stir with a whisk or fork until combined.

- Add flour, banana, sour cream or yogurt to the creamed mixture. Mix gently, just until combined. Use a spoon or rubber/vinyl spatula (don't overmix).

- Pour batter into prepared pan. Bake for 50-60 minutes. Test cake after 50 minutes.

- Remove cake from oven. Place on a cake rack or 2 table knives to cool. Cool for 10 minutes. Turn out onto a plate. Peel off waxed paper.

Serves 6

ORANGE BUTTER ICING – In a small bowl, using an electric mixer, beat 2 tbsp. (30 mL) **soft butter or margarine**, 2 cups (500 mL) **icing (confectioner's) sugar** and enough fresh or thawed frozen **orange juice** to make a spreadable icing, about 2-4 tbsp. (45-60 mL).

Variations

Add 1 cup (250 mL) toasted chopped **pecans** when you add the bananas, and frost the baked cake with **Orange Butter Icing**.

Cook's Tip

Most of the brand-name cake mix products are excellent. For convenience and good eating try the **chocolate** and **spice cake** versions and their variations. The **brownie** mixes are also very good.

INDEX

VERY VEGETARIAN INDEX

ACKNOWLEDGMENTS
– WITH MANY THANKS

Margo Embury, Publishing Director, Photo Designer and Food Stylist at Centax Books, for her ability to organize and format all that I wanted to say in this book and who, with the photographer, Patricia Holdsworth, produced the beautiful photos.

Iona Glabus, Publishing Assistant, for her formatting and attention to detail.

Kerry Ryan and Ellie Action for their word-processing skills and their patience with the revisions.

Allan, for his assistance in so many ways . . . taste testing to shipping and receiving.

Friends and family members who have offered encouragement and support for this book and for my first cookbook, *Quick Cooking for Busy People.*

My biggest thank you is for my children and grandchildren, who have led me to believe that I have done something special.

Quick Cooking
for Busy People
families—first-time cooks—singles

Prepare good healthy meals in less time than it takes to have a pizza delivered! Save time – save money – enjoy great food and good nutrition.

Perfect for busy families; ideal for university students and anyone setting up a first apartment; pared-down cooking for singles, this cookbook is designed for everyday use.

A comprehensive collection of starters, snacks, lunches and light meals, side dishes, main meals and desserts, most recipes also include quick and easy variations. Today, smart cooking for busy people incorporates the best ingredients (some fresh, some frozen, some canned), the fastest methods (some one-dish specials, some super-quick ideas), the most ingenious shortcuts (including some inspired deli and other instant add-ons). With a little planning and preparation, these meals can be ready in 30 minutes. There are also super-quick recipes throughout the book and a Super-Quick Meals and Snacks section.

Stress-free simple meal preparation is the goal of *Quick Cooking*. The best thing is – this food doesn't taste stress-free or quick or shortcut – it tastes great. With *Quick Cooking*, we can meet the challenges of everyday meal preparation. This collection of satisfying recipes, practical time and energy-saving tips can eliminate the daily dinner deadline panic.

Share *Quick Cooking for Busy People* and *Straight A's College Cookbook*

Order *Quick Cooking for Busy People* at $14.95 per book and
Straight A's College Cookbook at $18.95 per book, plus $4.00 (total order) for postage and handling.

Quick Cooking for Busy People _____ x $14.95 = $_____
Straight A's College Cookbook _____ x $18.95 = $_____
Shipping and handling (total order) _____ = $ 4.00
Subtotal _____ = $_____
In Canada add 7% GST _____ = $_____
Total enclosed _____ = $_____

$12.95 U.S. and international orders, payable in U.S. funds. U.S. shipping $4.00.
Price is subject to change.

NAME: _____
STREET: _____
CITY: _____ PROV./STATE: _____
COUNTRY: _____ POSTAL CODE/ZIP: _____

Please make cheque or money order payable to:
Sandy Hook Publishing
Box 202, Sandy Hook, Manitoba, Canada R0C 2W0
Telephone: 204-389-2005

For fund raising or volume purchase prices, contact Sandy Hook Publishing.
Please allow 3-4 weeks for delivery.

Share *Quick Cooking for Busy People* and *Straight A's College Cookbook*

Order *Quick Cooking for Busy People* at $14.95 per book and
Straight A's College Cookbook at $18.95 per book, plus $4.00 (total order) for postage and handling.

Quick Cooking for Busy People _____ x $14.95 = $_____
Straight A's College Cookbook _____ x $18.95 = $_____
Shipping and handling (total order) _____ = $ 4.00
Subtotal _____ = $_____
In Canada add 7% GST _____ = $_____
Total enclosed _____ = $_____

$12.95 U.S. and international orders, payable in U.S. funds. U.S. shipping $4.00.
Price is subject to change.

NAME: _____
STREET: _____
CITY: _____ PROV./STATE: _____
COUNTRY: _____ POSTAL CODE/ZIP: _____

Please make cheque or money order payable to:
Sandy Hook Publishing
Box 202, Sandy Hook, Manitoba, Canada R0C 2W0
Telephone: 204-389-2005

For fund raising or volume purchase prices, contact Sandy Hook Publishing.
Please allow 3-4 weeks for delivery.